CHANGING ON THE INSIDE

*The Keys to Spiritual Recovery
and Lasting Change*

John White

eagle

Guildford, Surrey

British Library Cataloguing in Publication Data. A catalogue
record for this book is available from the British Library.

First published in the USA in 1991 by Servant Publications,
Michigan.

Published in the UK by Eagle, an imprint of Inter Publishing
Service (IPS) Ltd, St Nicholas House, 14 The Mount, Guildford,
Surrey GU2 5HN. First printing 1991
Reprinted 1991
Reprinted 1992
Reprinted 1993
Reprinted 1994
Reprinted 1996

Printed by.Caledonian Interntional Book Manufacturing.
ISBN No: 0 86347 180 3

Contents

ONE

An Inner Revolution

Can the Ethiopian change his skin or the leopard its spots? Jeremiah 13:23

NOVELIST MORRIS WEST, in his gripping book, *Lazarus*, tells the story of a pope who undergoes a heart bypass operation and comes out a changed man. Formerly rigid and doctrinaire, this protagonist emerges from his brush with death a reformer—bent on humanizing both the Vatican and the whole Catholic church.

It's a dramatic, intriguing story. But could it really happen? Or does such a metamorphosis happen only in fiction?

In other words, can human beings really change, really turn their lives around?

My answer, based on long experience as a psychiatrist, writer, and student of human nature, is *yes*.

Deep, lasting change really is possible. And I don't just mean altered behavior, but a turnaround at the core of a person's being. A change so dramatic and decisive, we could call it an *inner revolution*.

I have seen it happen. As dynamic and miraculous as a sunrise or the birth of a baby, I always watch someone undergoing such a revolution with bemused wonder. The same wonder shines in the eyes of those who are changing—as though they are seeing the world for the first time.

1

At times people shake their heads saying, "I just never realized... " Something has happened deep inside, and changes in behavior and lifestyle soon follow. Just as new babies develop daily, a series of growth spurts are visible. The person is never the same again.

It happened to Chuck Colson. An arrogant and ambitious pragmatist, he was willing to do almost anything to advance his goal of getting Richard Nixon elected President. But in August 1973, following a revolution of the sort I am describing, Chuck Colson became a profoundly religious man. (We will look more deeply into his story in the next chapter.) Following a jail sentence for alleged complicity in the Watergate scandal, Chuck began an unexpected second career as a powerful advocate of prison reform. This man set out down a new road, and he has never turned back.

What happened to Colson has happened again and again to people in widely varying circumstances. Let's look at a few of them to get a broad picture of how these inner revolutions work:

BORN-AGAIN MAOISTS

In 1951, while still a medical student, I met a man with an intriguing story to tell. David Adeney had just returned from a stint in China, where he had served as Associate General Secretary for the Chinese Inter-Varsity movement, an evangelical Christian organization. His tenure was during the time when the Maoists were taking over the universities. I found Adeney's account of their techniques both fascinating and disturbing.

Adeney described mass meetings strangely similar to Christian evangelism techniques of the nineteenth and twentieth centuries. The Maoists began with choruses—catchy songs about the revolution that everyone was encouraged to sing. Once the meeting had been warmed up, students gave what used to be called "popcorn testimonies." These brief, enthusiastic accounts of their conversion to Mao's teachings included before-and-after descriptions of the students' former beliefs and actions, their struggles to know what to believe, and the impact of the new "gospel" of Mao's little red book. These converts to Maoism shared the joy and wonder of discovering the real "truth," and the sense of purpose and liberation that followed. They had found a life worth living, a life that contrasted starkly with their former selfishness and confusion. Their joy and enthusiasm were contagious.

Skilled and experienced communist orators spoke next, using the same emotional techniques employed by Western evangelists: ringing proclamations, earnest entreaties, even jokes to relax the students and put them at ease. And then came the appeals to change. Carried by the emotional tide of the gathering, the students lost touch with their emotional and intellectual bearings. Trained Maoist counselors—sometimes two or three to one inquiring student—helped individuals reach a commitment to the party. David Adeney felt that the joy and new purpose experienced by these new Maoists seemed to be just as real—and just as lasting—as that of newly converted Christians. The emotion might not last forever, but the commitment to the party following such "conversions" was neither ephemeral nor temporary. The new Maoists really *had* changed.

BETTY AND THE BATTLE WITH BOOZE

Change—even decisive change—is not always sudden. It wasn't for Betty, a recovering alcoholic. Remembering her experience, she says, "Some people walk into an Alcoholics Anonymous meeting and know instantly. They walk through the door—and it's a miracle. But it wasn't like that with me. I was in, out, in, out..."

Betty has become a member of our family by a kind of

mutual adoption. A vivacious, attractive, black-haired woman in her forties, she possesses a warmth and a sense of humor that have helped her survive a life of exceptional difficulty. Betty's first husband was an alcoholic. Her second, a man on whom she mistakenly took pity, made several attempts to murder her and finally committed suicide. Much later, one of her two sons was shot to death in a random street incident.

Betty has had more than her share of pain—some her own doing, some not. And even her trek to recovery has been a slow, stumbling one. But she has persisted, and today she has been sober for thirteen years.

Betty started to drink during the 1970s, while still in her first marriage.

"How did it start?" I asked her.

"I started to hate God's guts," she replied. "My sister's little boy, David, had a tumor. I prayed for him for a year—literally night and day. It never entered my head that he would not recover. But when David died, I became an atheist. Once I gave up on God, it was straight down the tube. I was drinking out of control right from the start."

"How long did it take you to realize you were an alcoholic?"

"I knew I was in trouble when I stopped making meals for my sons. I had worked so hard as a mother. It wasn't very long before I realized alcohol was becoming more important to me than Bobbie and Jamie. There would be no food on the table. While I was drinking, I stopped caring."

"And when you did try to quit, you weren't able to?"

"No. They say in AA that if you had a strong religious faith and lost it, you'll be a much tougher nut to crack. That was me. I read every how-to book I could lay my hands on, but I couldn't change. I thought I'd never change."

But Betty did change, through "working the Twelve Steps," the Alcoholics Anonymous path to sobriety. An integral part of that transformation involved coming to terms with the God she no longer believed in—in AA terms, "God as you understand him." Betty remembers: "At first I said, 'No way!' Then I began to pray, 'I know you're not there, and I know you're not gonna help me, but I'm told I've gotta do this.'"

Gradually, Betty began to change. She shakes her head wonderingly. "You know, God'll run with whatever you give him. It was still a struggle, but I began to realize that he *was* helping me."

There were "dozens of slips," then a two-year "dry" period, followed in 1977 by a further slip. That seems to have been the last. Today, Betty is an AA counselor, and she continues to work on her recovery one day at a time.

THE BIG MAN ON CAMPUS

Ward Gasque is a big man in his profession. A professor and administrator, he is widely sought for his flair and creativity in developing new academic institutions.

Ward is also a big man physically—so big that, several years ago, his doctors became worried. Ward was carrying four hundred twenty-eight pounds on his six-foot, seven-inch frame. He showed signs of early diabetes, and his cholesterol level had begun to climb.

Ward enjoyed food, wine, and the "good things in life." His family history encouraged overeating. The only child of moderately wealthy, older parents, Ward had been overindulged. He remembers that his mother in particular "was constantly pushing things in my mouth. I belonged to the clean plate club." Ward's mother was herself overweight, and as a boy he would occasionally discover (and consume) the candy bars she had hidden in different places in the house.

No wonder the boy grew up with a weight problem! But with enough other qualities contributing to his success in life, Ward's weight did not trouble him—until the specter of medical complications loomed.

"You are not in serious danger at this point," a doctor finally told him, "but you will be unless you change your lifestyle." Ward knew he had arrived at a crisis point. His physician underlined that fact as he preached a gentle gospel of a changed lifestyle during four successive visits. For the first time in his life, Ward listened.

Ward need not follow a rigid diet, the doctor said, but he would have to make some changes in what he ate and how much he exercised. Ward learned that while he could eat certain foods in almost unlimited quantities, he should consume others only in moderate amounts and avoid still others altogether. He would still be able to find pleasure in food, but he needed to focus on different foods.

His doctor insisted that Ward keep an accurate record of what he ate. This exercise helped Ward take a long, hard look at his eating habits—and showed him how difficult it is to remain honest. In a letter to friends he wrote, "It took a month to begin to be wholly honest with myself and to come to grips with the full impact of what I was faced with in black and white."

Would he—*could* he—stick with the sort of changed lifestyle his doctor recommended? Ward was uncertain. He had often tried to diet in the past, but with limited—and temporary—success. "The usual diet," he told me, "demands a degree of discipline I just don't have." Each failure deepened Ward's belief that he was not the sort of person who could permanently lose weight.

Despite his doubts, Ward knew with nagging certainty that if he failed to lose weight, his health would suffer. With diabetes, high blood pressure, and coronary artery disease seemingly just around the corner, Ward decided his life would change. And he hit on a motivational plan that was in keeping with his overall creativity.

Since he was well known in certain circles, Ward decided

to draw on this celebrity. He wrote letters to friends, colleagues, and acquaintances, asking them to back him in his weight-loss effort by giving money for each pound he lost during a three-month period. "Once you go public," he said, "you're committed."

Spurred on by his public commitment, Ward really did change. In those first three months, he took off sixty-three pounds. Then he lost seventy more—one hundred thirty-three pounds in all. Ward learned to focus on what he *could* eat, not what was forbidden, and to eat three meals a day, with carefully chosen snacks. Fond of milkshakes in summer, he learned to enjoy a concoction of unsweetened frozen strawberries whipped with skimmed milk. Taking long walks on a regular basis helped him learn to appreciate the natural beauty around him.

Five years have passed since Ward began his weight-loss effort. For a long time he maintained his new weight, but in recent months he has put on ten pounds. Ward watches himself more carefully now, determined not to return to the danger that once threatened him.

PUTTING A MIDLIFE CRISIS TO WORK

I meet one every week or so—a person whose direction has changed dramatically in midlife. Executives pack in their careers and take to sailing yachts around the world. Married men and women embark on affairs after years of fidelity. Business owners sell out and go back to school, determined to "do something they like" the second time around.

And then there is Tom. Short, pot-bellied, genial, he still owns a successful construction business—but he has found his deepest satisfaction elsewhere. Several years ago, Tom became aware of a gnawing discontent in his life. He was a dedicated churchgoer, a Catholic, but there seemed to be an enormous difference between his power and effectiveness in his business and his meaningless, passive role in the church. Even Tom's business successes seemed impotent to bring him the "something else" he was looking for in life. At one point Tom tried to express his frustration to his priest, but couldn't make himself understood. "All I did was hurt Father Callahan's feelings," Tom recalls.

Then Tom attended a lecture on the needs of missionary orders in certain African countries. "It was like lights going on in my head," he remembers. He sensed that message held the solution to his indefinable emotional needs. As he considered the possibilities, Tom began to see that employing his construction know-how in a missionary setting might be what he was looking for. Further talks with his priest and with the bishop opened his way to work in Africa, constructing small church buildings.

Tom turned the management of his business over to his brother, who had been assisting him all along. He gave himself a regular salary and poured his profits into this new work in Africa. Tom's children were young enough to adapt to radical change, and his wife was even more enthusiastic than he about the project. "I travel with him, and I see much more of him than I used to," she comments.

After five years, this business arrangement has not changed and Tom's enthusiasm for his new career remains strong. "I should have done this years before," he says.

CHANGE THAT TRANSFORMS A NATION

This inner revolution can be more sudden and dramatic than in any of the examples I have given. Moreover, it can affect large numbers of people at once, even turn a nation upside down. Such a revolution occurred in a remote valley of Wales in 1859.

The pastor of a little Calvinist Methodist church had preached a sermon which "got under people's skins." At the business meeting the following Wednesday, "the fur nearly flew"—but not quite. Someone at the meeting later recorded the events in his diary:

> One of the elders got up and said it was a very difficult thing for a man to say "Amen" under a ministry he felt condemning him; and as he said these things he sat down as if fainting away. At this moment, there was something (I cannot say what it was, but that it was *something* that neither I nor any one else had ever felt before) went through the whole congregation, until every one put down his head and wept! The following week the two churches, Wesleyan and Calvinistic Methodists, united to keep prayer meetings every night.... "[1]

During those moments, a revival of religion began, and it spread from that tiny village church to turn the whole country of Wales on its head.

The changes resulting from that Welsh revival were astonishing. Wales, for example, had been a hard-drinking country. Ordinary people suffered a difficult lot in those days—slaving in the mines or in factories and foundries for a pittance. Many men drank heavily to assuage the drudgery and hopelessness. Following the revival, however, such a transformation in the morale and the behavior swept through multitudes of people that nearly two-thirds of the public drinking houses closed for lack of business!

THE REVOLUTION WITHIN: FACTORS IN CHANGE

Inner revolutions that result in changed lifestyles do take place. I am by no means convinced that the changes in the accounts I have given involve identical inner processes. I certainly cannot predict with certainty which changes involving living persons will be permanent. But all of these stories do seem alike in some ways. Let's look at what these change-stories have in common and how they differ.

Ward, Chuck, Betty, the Chinese students, the Welsh people, and Tom all experienced profound changes in their lifestyles. Many of the changes were sudden and dramatic—but not all of them. Although Betty's descent was sudden and dramatic, for example, her return to sobriety was slow and halting.

Most of the changes described were positive—but, again, not all of them. Inner revolutions, it seems, can turn people in any direction—positive or negative. Colson and the Welsh villagers repented of their sins and turned toward God. The Chinese repented of being bourgeois and exchanged one tyrannical system for another. Betty experienced *two* revolutions. First, she got mad at God and "went straight down the tube." Later, she learned about herself through AA and found her way to maturity and sobriety.

All the changes appear to be lasting rather than superficial. However, the possibility for "backsliding" or even a second change of direction was always there. Betty and Ward have had to work hard to keep from falling back into their former lifestyles. Presumably, Chuck and Tom and the Chinese students had moments when they could have been in danger of turning back to their old ways.

Yet another common denominator of these stories is that the internal revolutions brought release from tension and/or imprisonment. The people involved were freed from the confines of their perverse nature and being—even if that sense of release turned out to be temporary or false. In many cases, however, their new freedom was neither temporary nor spurious, but real and lasting.

Most important, all of these changes involved a fundamental change in the person's *perception* of reality. They came to view life differently, and at some deep level they responded to that changed perception. All of their subsequent changes in behavior emanated from a willed response to their new view of reality. I see this changed perception as the essence of their inner revolution.

WHAT CHANGE IS GOOD CHANGE?

Changes in life direction interest me as a psychiatrist, as well as a Christian. What is their secret? What happens inside a person who changes? Is there a key to the change in lifestyle?

I am also interested in the value and the reality of the change that results. After all, revolutions do not always improve the situation. While violent political revolutions may relieve tension for a time, they commonly return affairs to a similar state in the long haul. The life of ordinary people in China has not greatly improved either economically or politically since the peasants' long march and the revolution. All the more reason then to know where the key lies to ongoing change for the better.

Change can be superficial—even easy—for some people. They seem to change directions in life the way other people change shoes. No internal revolution seems to be necessary. Such people have a kind of weather-vane personality which swings with the wind of fashion. Their entire lives are oriented toward novelty and intellectual fashion. They are *for* whatever happens to be *in*.

But in developmental terms, such people never *move*, but stay in the same spot all their lives. They take new directions without going anywhere. They haven't really changed at all; they only *appear* to have changed. That's not the kind of change I'm talking about. I am interested in change that is both *real* and *positive*. To be worthwhile, change has to have two characteristics: it must involve a lasting, positive change in life goals (and therefore in direction) and a consequent growth in personal maturity. Without the emotional maturity, the goals will never be reached, the new behavior will never be learned.

With this in mind, we will have to ask some questions about inner revolutions that lead to major lifestyle change. In particular, we need to ask what makes the resulting change *real*, *positive*, and *ongoing*.

This is not just a rhetorical question. So many people would like to change—really change, from the inside out. Some have reached the point of desperation, almost convinced there is no way out of their destructive situation.

In my work, I meet gays who feel resentful that they are not like other women and men. I meet addicts who long to be in control, spouse beaters and child abusers who feel powerless to stop hurting those they love. I meet people who despair of ever being in a healthy relationship, people who hunger for a more meaningful life, people who yearn to break habits that prevent them from being their best.

All these people have what psychologists and psychiatrists might call "ego dystonic" conditions—conditions that make them feel bad about themselves. Psychiatry and psychology are adept at *describing* the problems. They offer a variety of explanations and helping techniques, many of which are useful. But psychology and psychiatry have their limits. After years in therapy, many people remain convinced there is no way out, that they simply cannot change.

In this book, therefore, I want to take a fresh look at change in human behavior and to show how real, positive, lasting change *can* come about. I hope to do so with a minimum of psychological jargon. Fluency in jargon—sometimes referred to as psychobabble—creates the illusion that we know something, when all we really accomplish is to expertly navigate through an endless sea of fascinating words.

I also want to push beyond the limits of psychology—to dare consider the *spiritual* component that I believe is at the heart of any inner revolution. I don't want to sound overly mystical yet the inner change I am groping to describe does have a mystical, "meant to be" quality involving the progressive evolution of what I would like to call the *real person*.

It reminds me of the old Greek idea that freedom is rooted in design. According to this notion, all things are designed to function a certain way, and are most free when they function as they were designed to function. Fish are most free when they swim, for instance, and birds when they fly.

By this sort of reasoning, human beings are designed to do—what? The changes I am looking at in this book are inner changes that put human beings on the path toward becoming truly what they were *designed* to be. Understanding that kind of change—and helping it come about—*must* involve looking beyond surface behavior or even psychological dynamics.

THE REVOLUTION OF REPENTANCE

Another word for the inner revolution I'm talking about is *repentance*.

Repentance is not a popular word these days. We tend to associate it with the rantings of ancient prophets and with an arid, restricted view of life—deserts rather than growth.

But repentance is precisely the inner revolution I am talking about. It describes the deep, inner turning that makes real, lasting change possible. To be honest, repentance usually *does* come after some time in the "desert," some time of dry dissatisfaction or rocky pain. And yet it truly is the way to growth and regeneration. It is my conviction, in fact, that without repentance, real and lasting change is impossible.

But isn't *repentance* a religious term? Certainly, it has religious implications, and I will discuss many of them in the pages to come. But I find it more helpful to think of repentance as a uniquely *human* phenomenon, something that has to do with the way we are made. It hinges on the dilemma of being a human being in a world where pleasures and joys mingle with evil, tragedy, and cruelty. It comes into play in turning some people to Communism, as surely as it does in turning others to Christianity.

Repentance is something that would interest any good psychiatrist, religious or not. Of course, it is something religious people usually do in churches or religious places before an altar or at a penitents' bench. Jews in the Old Testament and both Jews and Gentiles in the New Testament were repeatedly told to repent.

There are even Greek and Hebrew terms for it, like *metanoia* and *nocham*—and books written to explain their precise nuances. *Metanoia* refers to a changed way of viewing or perceiving matters. *Nocham* has (among other connotations) the sense of entering into comfort. These terms, describing as they do many centuries of human reality, can be helpful in explaining this uniquely human phenomenon of repentance.

Let me then attempt to define repentance and, as I do so, the fundamental nature of the inner revolution. It seems to begin with a profound change in the way we see reality. This changed perception is not merely an intellectual change, or what psychologists refer to as a *cognitive* change.[2] It is one thing, after all, to "know" we're going to die some day, and quite another to be confronted with lethal danger.

The changed perception of repentance is more like that second experience. It involves the shock of "seeing" some aspect of reality for the first time. Consider reading a book about diving and "knowing" that a dive from the high diving board could be a little scary, as compared with standing on a high diving board for the first time—while a line of other would-be divers waits behind you.

Because repentance involves such a deep-seated recognition of reality, emotions quickly become involved. I suspect the depth of emotion is related to the depth and permanence of the change—hence the weeping of the Welsh people and the efforts by Communist orators to rouse emotional confusion in Chinese students.

But repentance must also involve volition (the will)—volition of a sort that is more than an intellectual decision to change. For years, Ward Gasque and Betty struggled ineffectively to change, in spite of all their best resolutions. Then, at some point something happened at a deeper level—perhaps we should say at an *unconscious* level—that involved their wills. Somewhere deep inside, when confronted with a different view of reality, they responded with a will to change. Deep within, they changed direction. Behavioral changes inevitably followed that down-deep decision. Is repentance the same as change? They are related, but not synonymous. Repentance refers to the inner revolution—the combination of changed perception and willed response—that must take place before lasting change is possible. Repentance precedes behavioral change; it paves the way. It is the underlying mechanism that gives rise to changed behavior. In my view, it is the *only* mechanism that offers true hope for healthy and permanent change.

HOW DOES IT HAPPEN?

How does it all work? More to the point, how can it work for you and for those you care about?

Those are the questions this book will address. More specifically, this book will seek to answer the following questions:

1. *How does this inner revolution happen?* What order of events leads to a fundamental turnaround? We will examine this in chapter two.
2. *What determines whether change is truly deep, positive, and*

lasting? Chapter three will begin this focus, but the entire book will continue to elaborate on this question.

3. *What part do intellect, emotions, and will play in bringing about repentance and change?* And how do we cooperate in our own change? Chapters four through seven pick up this emphasis.

4. *What makes positive change an ongoing process?* How can we avoid "backsliding" or negative change, and continue to grow toward health and maturity? That will be the focus of chapters eight and nine.

5. *What role do persuasive techniques play in helping people change?* Where does enabling stop and manipulation begin? Chapter eight will address these questions, which have important implications for our "marketing centered" society as well as for Christian evangelism and witness.

6. Finally, *what is the nature of reality?* The question is often posed these days with a kind of joking despair, as if it were eternally beyond us. But since inner revolutions occur at such a deep level, understanding them demands digging down beyond behavioral or even psychological issues and confronting the true nature of reality—including good and evil.

Closely related to this issue of reality is the question of the supernatural. Much change is religious or spiritual in nature. Can such change be truly explained by science? Can science really explain the nineteenth-century Welsh revival or the effect of orators on the Chinese students?

The question of the nature of reality is specifically addressed in chapter three, but permeates the entire book as well. Because I have come to believe that real, lasting change always stems from a confrontation with reality, my own understanding of reality will necessarily play a part in my explanations.

Let me say at the outset, then, that I am a Christian. I am convinced that the most important inner revolution in any person's life is the moment of Christian repentance—of turning away from sin and toward God. And the truly life-giving change is that of accepting Christ into one's life.

At the same time, I believe that the mechanism that drives repentance is built into every human being, regardless of religious persuasion. That means that real, positive, and lasting change is available to non-Christians. And even those who have made a decision to follow Christ have a need for ongoing repentance and change in specific areas of their lives. Christians as well as non-Christians struggle with habits, behaviors, and attitudes that keep them from being all they were meant to be.

Real, positive, lasting change can happen only from within—in my view, only through the work of the Holy Spirit. And yet my experience shows that this transformation can be encouraged and helped along. Providing that kind of help and encouragement is the real purpose of this book.

TWO

Anatomy of an Earthquake

All things have second birth;
The earthquake is not satisfied at once.
William Wordsworth

INNER REVOLUTIONS that lead to lasting life-change may be sudden and unexpected, but they are never isolated events. Moments of repentance inevitably follow years—sometimes an entire lifetime—of inner and outer experiences leading toward the crisis moment, and changes continue to unfold long after the moment has passed.

The analogy of a revolution is actually a very good one. Years of discontent—stemming from economic hardship, political repression, domination by one group or another—finally result in upheaval. Heads roll. Fortunes change. Governments are reformed. Then, as months and years go by, the country tries to sort out what the future will be like.

Another good comparison might be one of those Japanese domino demonstrations. (I used to do the same sort of thing as a kid, but the Japanese have made it a national sport!) Patient volunteers take up to a year to set up hundreds, perhaps thousands of dominoes, each domino carefully positioned. Then when the first domino is tipped, the rest fall in rapid sequence, startling us by forming a pattern.

Inner revolutions, I believe, always follow a prolonged and silent arrangement of inner and outer events—an unconcious arrangement of dominoes. Then something equivalent to the tipping of the first domino occurs, and the rest follows.

Perhaps the best picture, however, is that of an earthquake. As I type this morning, deep in the earth beneath me here in Vancouver a vast plate of the earth's crust is pushing its way under the shoreline. A second plate—on the shore side—is bending downward as the first plate doubles it over. Or so seismologists and geologists tell us. Tension builds as the continental shelf creeps west, preparing us for an all-time great of an earthquake. The newspapers have threatened us with nine points on the Richter scale. No one can say when it will happen. But when it does, some definite changes will take place!

Change in people can result from a personal earthquake— as tension is released and the elements of life are rearranged.

How does such a personal earthquake proceed? My experience suggests that it happens in three phases. Phase one consists of the events leading up to the crisis. Phase two is the turning point itself, and phase three is the period of change that follows it. In this chapter, I want to explore these three phases—especially the first two—by using the example of Chuck Colson. His book, *Born Again*, which documents his own change experience in detail, gives us excellent material for understanding how an inner earthquake comes about.

PHASE ONE: BEFORE THE EARTHQUAKE

Phase one of an inner earthquake, which may be lifelong, involves a build-up of tensions—accumulating pressures that must eventually find release.

As I have indicated, real earthquakes result from a build-up of tensions deep in the earth. Far beneath the earth's surface, vast and massive plates of rock float over a fluid core. Surface land masses and ocean beds rest on these unstable foundations. The plates are not static but in motion—albeit slow and ponderous, usually undetected at the surface. Plate presses against plate with titanic power, creating pressures of incredible magnitude. Something eventually has to give, so that the relationships change.

The same is true of us as persons. We are conscious only of our surface lives, unable to see the powerful movements deep below our surface experiences. Tensions and pressures can develop of which we are unaware, at least for a time. We feel the results of the tensions, however, and are puzzled when our feelings do not correspond to our circumstances. Such is the influence of what psychoanalysts call our unconscious minds.

Conflicting pressures develop in us much as they do beneath the earth's surface. Certain tendencies within us conflict with other tendencies, and external events trigger changes in the balance of competing elements. Finally, at some point, the built-up tension reaches a crisis point. "Something gives," as we say, and from the depths below comes a rending and a shaking.

The unconscious forces that lead to a personal earthquake normally are hidden from us. A skilled helper—a good psychologist or psychiatrist—may help them to surface. However, the unconscious material may also come to light without anyone's intervention. This was the case with Chuck Colson. His understanding of the pattern of events impinging on his life—as well as the inner battle they had provoked—came about through hours of reflection while in prison.

Years after his personal "earthquake," Colson came to see that his inner tension began with several ingrained character traits. On one hand there was his pride, the financial insecurity of his boyhood, and his awareness of the contempt of

Boston's "Brahmins" for people like himself. Opposing these was the example and teaching of his father, and a political idealism he had somehow internalized early in life.

Colson believes that *pride* was a driving force in his life from an early age. In *Born Again*, he recalls the speech he gave as valedictorian of his high-school class: "We are proud, very proud... of the school—of our class."[1] Later, he was to realize that being proud was his chief weakness, and to conclude that this pride was morally evil.

Insecurity is the other face of pride. Chuck's father had struggled through years of night school during the depression to qualify both as an accountant and as a lawyer. Inevitably Chuck became aware of the uncertainty of life. "Being in debt, being unsure where next month's rent would come from, created an insecurity which... doubtless fueled my later drive to achieve."[2]

But the insecurity had other roots besides the economic uncertainties of his boyhood. "As a boy I used to stand on the pebbly beach looking across the gray-green waters of the harbor at the city then run by the Brahmins, the Beacon Hill establishment which traced its ancestry through generations of Harvard classes back to the Mayflower." Chuck did not belong to a Brahmin family. "'Swamp Yankees' we were called," he says, "Acceptance was what we were denied—and what we most fervently sought."[3]

His insecurity was the insecurity of rejection, as well as that of economic uncertainty. It was class rejection, the knowledge that one is looked down on by a superior class.

When insecurity fueled by ambition is combined with an awareness of being looked down upon by a superior class, the result is potentially explosive tension. This tension continued to build in Chuck throughout his long career. Proud and ambitious, Chuck even rejected a full scholarship Harvard awarded him. "In my pride I believed I had something better—the chance to turn them down. It was warped pride, no doubt, but the resentment against Eastern intellectualism stayed with me and shaped some of the tumultuous events of my later life."[4]

Militating against these tendencies was the early influence of his father. Colson's father was a good father who both modeled and taught sacrifice, truthful integrity, and hard work as keys to progress in life. This visible model was more important than the teaching in passing along these ideals to Chuck.

A good parent can largely determine what we call the *ego ideals* of his or her child. "Ego ideal" translates as *the kind of person I would like to be*, the sort of person I would like to look at in the mirror of truth. Many of us are in tension because our ego ideal conflicts with tendencies deep within us. For instance, many alcoholics don't care for the picture they have of themselves, because it violates their ego ideal. "Henpecked" husbands may despise their wimpiness for the same reason.

Colson's father combined his hard working example with instruction. "Work hard," he told Chuck. "Study hard; nothing comes easy in this life. There are no short cuts. No matter how menial the job you have, the important thing is to do it well."[5]

More significantly, Colson's father was concerned about truthfulness. "Tell the truth," he would say, "Tell the truth—always—lies destroy you."[6] The advice, which his son struggled to follow faithfully, would create further inner tensions as his political career unfolded.

It is not clear how Colson's political idealism arose. Perhaps it was his father's pride in the land of opportunity. Perhaps the childhood rhetoric of liberty and patriotism had entrenched a belief in the system deep inside his nature. At any rate, Chuck was firmly convinced that good government was the key to national greatness and harmony. Only later did he realize that national greatness, harmony, prosperity arose from the character and the attitude of the country's citizens, and that "a country gets the government it deserves."

THE TENSIONS MOUNT

Early experiences in Chuck Colson's career played on his basic character traits to accelerate the build-up of inner tension. As a volunteer worker for the Republican party in Boston, he acquired "an education in practical politics, Boston-style. I learned all the tricks, some of which went up to and even slightly over the legal boundaries. Phony mailings, tearing down opposition signs, planting misleading stories in the press, voting tombstones, and spying out the opposition in every possible way were all standard fare."[7]

Gradually Colson began to develop a political toughness—even a ruthlessness—that helped further his political ambitions, but brought him inner conflict because it contradicted his father's teaching. Much later, during the time when Chuck served Richard Nixon as his special assistant, the President wrote Colson's father expressing his appreciation of his son, and his gratitude for his services. His father in turn wrote to Chuck, claiming the letter was his most treasured possession. But that letter made Chuck Colson squirm: "Abruptly, I picked up the letter and thrust it into a drawer. I knew, as Dad did not, that if I was as valuable to the President as he said I was, it was because I was willing at times to blink at certain ethical standards, to be ruthless in getting things done. It was earning me status and power... "[8]

Let me again stress the significance of a close father-son relationship. The desire to gain even an indifferent father's approval motivates much of what a son does. His sexuality, his sense of manhood, his approach to marriage, the way he rears his children, his attitude to his career—all are influenced by that need. The letter, therefore, left a sour taste in

Colson's mouth. It was a painful reminder that the status Colson hungered for was being gained by means of ethical standards his father deplored.

Tensions were building at the very root of Colson's nature. Scorn-fueled ambition was clashing with the deepest of all longings in a man—the longing to win (without any cheating) his father's approval and to be as good, or even better, a man.

Disappointment with his political ambitions threatened to break into Colson's consciousness. But he resisted. Instead, he did the same thing with his need to please his father that he was already doing with his conscience—he buried it.

An old friend had once encouraged him to just walk around and enjoy the beauty of the White House and the grounds. "Take deep breaths and sniff in the history. It will help you to remember where you are and keep things in perspective." By nature ambitious and energetic—perhaps even a workaholic—Chuck's days and nights had made such advice impossible to follow. Crisis after crisis found him with no time to think of anything but the survival of the administration. He writes, "I was aware of where I was, all right, but somehow the perspective had not come. The past months had been too frantic."[9]

Later on, in the face of public disapproval of Nixon's decisions, what Colson calls a "fortress mentality" began to plague the Nixon administration. Morality is rooted in the joy of inner wholeness, in the glad certainty that you are doing what you were made to do. Moral chaos can spread quickly in government when fear and hate envelop an administration: "Our fortress mentality plunged us across a moral divide, leading to 'enemy lists,' a new refinement on the ancient spoils system of rewarding friends and punishing enemies. Other excesses came, as the shadowy form of the demon which was to strike down the thirty-seventh President of the United States was now slowly taking shape—like a genie drifting out of a bottle."[10]

Chuck was trapped. He had been an advocate of getting things done—unethically if need be. Now he was at the heart of this administration, his ruthless pragmatism an essential component of its modus operandi. Moreover, his presence in that strategic position was the gateway to his ambition to outclass the Brahmins.

But Chuck had never quite lost the belief that people mattered. The horror of what had happened at Kent State University—when the National Guard fired on students protesting Nixon's order to invade Cambodia—awoke that feeling within him again. He was a father. He knew what his own children meant to him. Along with other staffers, he watched the grim pictures on a White House TV screen in stunned silence. In an taped interview, the father of a dead girl charged, "The President is to blame!" Chuck recalls:

> My first reaction was: How unfair! What a terrible thing to say. The President didn't have anything to do with Allison's death. And then I thought, *Supposing it were my Emily?* I, too, would lash out at the leader of the government.... Maybe I'd do more.
>
> Then the sickening thought crossed my mind that if his accusation was fair, even in part, then I, too, was responsible; I'd helped the President make the Cambodia decision....
>
> I learned in time that if I was to remain in the White House, advising the President on decisions which meant life and death to real people, I could afford no personal feelings.[11]

It was an attitude that could not last. It could not resist the power of other forces deep within him. The following diagram summarizes the tensions that were mounting deep inside Chuck Colson. An earthquake of his own soul was becoming inevitable.

The Factors Summarized

Let us look at a simple diagram below illustrating the build up of tensions.

The Components of the Tension:

early financial insecurity ────────┐
insecurity from class consciousness ⟩──→ FIERCE AMBITION
personal pride ─────────────────┘

political idealism ──────────────→ LOVE OF POLITICS

father's modelling and teaching of
truthfulness, integrity, hard work ─────┐
instinctive feelings about real people ─┘──→ EGO IDEAL

The Anatomy of the Tension:

FIERCE AMBITION ─┐
LOVE OF POLITICS ─┘─→ growing tension ←─ EGO IDEAL

THE LAST STRAW: DISENCHANTMENT

The earthquake might never have taken place if power and status had continued to dazzle Colson. And for a long time, the perks of power were enough to keep the tensions in place. For years, he was able to push down his innate misgivings into his unconscious mind. Only incidents such as thrusting his father's letter into a drawer revealed that there was any tension at all. And his psychological mechanisms were able to handle such tensions—for his star was still rising.

President Nixon wanted to win another election. He saw that Chuck Colson would be an essential element in winning what would not be an easy campaign. The man who had enabled Nixon to get his own way during his first term of office might have the magic to enable him to win another election campaign.

So the day came when Chuck and his wife, Patty, rode at Nixon's invitation in the President's private compartment of the helicopter, *Air Force One*, bound for a private weekend in Key Biscayne. Colson recalls: "Nixon's gesture—seemingly so casual—the two families riding together—was a signal to the staff and the press travelling with us: I was to be in charge of the political game plan. At that moment I felt a sense of victory and even immunity from the petty bickering and infighting in the White House. It was the last time I was to feel that kind of elation."[12]

The election campaign was exciting, and the outcome a victory for the Republicans. By the time the victorious results came in, however, Chuck had lost the enthusiasm with which he had plunged into the battle. As he looked around him at the celebration party, he sensed a "sour" atmosphere in the Washington ballroom: "Patty turned to me. 'What's wrong, Chuck? You're so quiet.' 'I don't *know* what's wrong. Just exhausted, I guess.'"[13]

Exhausted he may have been. But more than exhaustion accounted for his mood. If Chuck had seen signs of a better America in people's behavior that night, things might have been different. If he had found a room full of joy and unselfish dedication, his exhaustion would have mattered little. His intense effort, his willingness to sacrifice ethical principles and also to tolerate the bickering among the White House staff had been bolstered by the conviction that he and Nixon were working to improve the country.

What Colson saw and heard at the party began to undermine that confidence. A "throng pushing and shoving four deep around the bar" was only interested in free drinks. VIPs were making petty complaints about Nixon. Party hangers-on unsmilingly besieged Chuck for jobs. The upbeat attitudes that had characterized the party's 1968 victory were nowhere to be found. The incident caused a pre-earthquake tremor:

> No, I wasn't imagining the sour mood. But something was also wrong in me. My insides were as deadened as the air in the room and the slow beat of the music.... Being part of electing a president was the fondest ambition of my life. For three long years I had committed everything I had, every ounce of energy to Richard Nixon's cause. Nothing else had mattered. We had had no time together as a family, no social life, no vacations. So why could my tongue not taste the flavor of his conquest?[14]

Chuck Colson was beginning to see that politics did not change people, that you need better people if you are to have a better America. Even so, had the man he worked for portrayed himself in a better light that same night, Chuck Colson might still have avoided the crisis that was to turn his personal world around. Chuck had idealized the President, seeing more virtues in him than he may have possessed. Nixon, who in previous years had shown himself magnanimous in defeat, now seemed to Chuck to be selfish and petty in victory.

As the tensions built deep inside Colson, he began to feel changes within himself. He felt tired, depleted, like "an exhausted volcano." During a trip to Camp David, he realized that something was seriously wrong with him. He describes his arrival there along with Peter Brennan, a trade-union friend. Luxury seemed wedded to military efficiency in the security measures with which they were received at the presidential retreat. Peter was impressed, but Chuck, who was accustomed to the scene, just felt depressed: "'This place is not for me,' I said. 'I feel like I'm being watched all the time, guards everywhere, even hiding behind the trees. It's like one of those secret hideaways in a James Bond movie—eerie! I can't wait to get back to the city.'"

"Brennan was staring at me. 'Chuck, you need a rest. Something's bugging you.' "[15]

Soon after the election, Chuck left the Nixon administration. He had advised the President of his intentions long before. A job in his old law firm, now greatly expanded, awaited him. The firm even gave him a new Lincoln Continental with a hired driver as a welcome-back present. Important clients were lining up to consult with him. He writes, "All of this, the warm welcome, plenty of money, surely... would give me new thrust."[16]

The new thrust did not come. Tiredness increased. The depression deepened.[17] The earthquake could come at any time.

In the way I have presented it, the process leading up to Chuck Colson's moment of repentance may seem merely automatic and predetermined. I do not believe it is. In our two-dimensional, naturalistic thinking, we sometimes fail to take any account of the divine Spirit who guides our destinies. The Spirit's aim, I believe, is to bring us to the fullness of our personhood and to an understanding of all he designed us to be and to do. I am convinced that Spirit was guiding Chuck with deft maneuvers. Our growth, even the tensions building to repentance, is part of this guided process of becoming. I hope in future chapters to make a convincing argument for that process and to show something of how it comes about.

PHASE TWO: CRISIS

After this long build-up, Chuck Colson's earthquake finally hit. Let's look at Colson's own description of what I have variously referred to as the crisis, the inner revolution, the earthquake, and repentance.

It is August 12, 1973. Colson has just spent time with Tom

Phillips, president of Raytheon Company, the largest employer in New England. Phillips is one of Colson's clients, and has just recounted to him the story of a revolution in his own life. Sensing Chuck may be interested, he reads a chapter to him from C.S. Lewis' book *Mere Christianity*—a chapter about pride. This tough politician finds his body heat rising as Lewis's words bite into his jaded political conscience.

Colson starts reviewing his life and is appalled by what he sees: "I could feel a flush coming into my face and a curious burning sensation that made the night seem even warmer. Lewis's words seem to pound right at me.... Suddenly I felt naked and unclean, my bravado defenses gone. I was exposed, unprotected, for Lewis's words were describing me... Now, sitting there on the dimly lit porch, my self-centered past was washing over me in waves. It was painful. Agony.... "[18]

Years later, Chuck would read C.S. Lewis' description of repentance and recognize what had happened to him: "It is something much harder than merely eating humble pie. It means unlearning all the self-conceit and self-will that we have been training ourselves into for thousands of years. It means killing part of yourself, undergoing a kind of death.[19]

For the moment, however, all he feels is the pain.

Pain, the real pain of the exposure of one's naked wretchedness, is inherent in the process of repentance. I believe it is because of the pain—and the accompanying turmoil which he experiences—that Chuck refuses further help from Phillips. At that point he is afraid of his own reactions. He is a man. He has been taught that a man can handle his own emotions. So Chuck declines an invitation to discuss the reading with Tom Phillips, courteously thanks his host, and takes his leave.

Colson gets into his car in the driveway and gropes in the dark for the ignition key, only to find that "manhood" and control are not enough. He begins to weep. Chuck Colson's personal earthquake has begun.

The realization grips him that he has made a mistake. He

should have stayed and talked to Phillips. But as he gets out of the car to return to the house, he thinks it is too late. The lights are being extinguished one by one while he stands beside the car. He gets back in and starts the motor:

As I drove out of Tom's driveway, the tears were flowing uncontrollably. There were no street lights, no moonlight. The car headlights were flooding illumination before my eyes, but I was crying so hard it was like trying to swim underwater. I pulled to the side of the road not more than a hundred yards from the entrance to Tom's driveway, the tires sinking into soft mounds of pine needles.

I remember hoping that Tom and Gert wouldn't hear my sobbing, the only sound other than the chirping of crickets penetrating the still of the night. With my face cupped in my hands, head leaning forward against the wheel, I forgot about machismo, about pretenses, about fears of being weak. And as I did, I began to experience a wonderful feeling of being released. Then came the strange sensation that water was not only running down my cheeks, but surging through my whole body as well, cleansing and cooling as it went. They weren't tears of sadness or remorse, nor of joy—but somehow tears of relief.

And then I prayed my first real prayer. "God, I don't know how to find You, but I'm going to try! I'm not much the way I am now, but somehow I want to give myself to You." I didn't know how to say more, so I repeated over and over the words: Take me.

I had not "accepted" Christ—I still didn't know who He was. My mind told me it was important to find that out first, to be sure that I knew what I was doing, that I meant it and would stay with it. Only, that night, something inside me was urging me to surrender—to what or whom I did not know.

I stayed there in the car, wet-eyed, praying, thinking,

for perhaps half an hour, perhaps longer, alone in the quiet of the dark night. Yet for the first time in my life I was not alone at all.[20]

Colson was not experiencing a "nervous breakdown" or "burnout" triggered by overwork or accumulated tensions. The fact that something more profound was happening is attested to by his subsequent switch in values, career, and lifestyle. A radical change was taking place in the depth of his character. An earthquake had shaken the foundations of his being. In later years, an entire country would witness the changed topography of his life.

WHAT HAPPENED IN THE EARTHQUAKE

We can note several interesting features of this earthquake that has cracked open Chuck Colson's crusty exterior. For one thing, profound emotion accompanies it. Pain precedes and introduces it, along with a curious sensation of bodily burning.

For another, a sense of release and peace follows immediately, even though Chuck has not yet understood what is happening to him. The tensions that have been building up for so many years are now relieved. There is also a feeling that he is being washed, that water is flowing over his being.

Later, we will note that a shift has taken place in his view of himself and of the world: he sees reality a different way. This readjustment of outlook is a vital component of any form of repentance, and the substance of that new vision is what determines whether the change is positive.

For now, however, Chuck is aware only that *for the first time in his life* he is no longer alone. He senses a presence with him, a presence that spells peace. It is almost as though he and his father-image were together again—except the Presence seems more like the Father of fatherhood itself.

We should note, however, that the earthquake has not turned Chuck into a Christian. Although it has certainly prepared him for conversion, he has at this point accepted no ideology or belief system. All he knows is that the presence he senses is worth trying to pray to. Repentance precedes belief systems.

AA members who remain dry have usually been through something equivalent to Chuck's earthquake—either in a series of "shocks" or in one "big one." For a surprising number of AA members, this can lead to Christian conversion. For most AA members, it does not do so. In either case, the psychological mechanism of repentance is the same.

Christians make a great to-do about conversion, by which we commonly mean both acceptance of a belief system and personal commitment to and trust in the person of Jesus Christ. Conversion hinges on *faith*, and faith itself involves more than an intellectual assent to certain doctrines.

However, without repentance—that is, without this type of mysterious earthquake—true faith is not possible. The earthquake of repentance is the doorway to faith and to behavior change. It is the beginning of true enlightenment.

PHASE 3: THE ONGOING EARTHQUAKES

The effects of an earthquake do not end when the earth stops shaking. Once the topography has been permanently altered, the ongoing process of discovering what life is like in that changed environment must begin.

Moreover, the underlying forces that produced the quake in the first place have not disappeared. They continue their underground pushing and shoving. For days and even weeks afterward come inevitable aftershocks, and the possibility of new tremors always exits.

The same is true for repentance. It is a way of life which involves a lifelong series of "aftershocks" and "tremors"—as release succeeds release, change succeeds change, and one degree of maturity succeeds another.

Colson's own "ongoing earthquake" involved a sequence of events. First, he did become a Christian. Through involvement with a group of Christian men, along with much study and meditation, he formed a solid belief system. Sentenced to prison for his part in the Watergate scandal, he began to make extensive notes about his own experience, while developing a deep compassion for his fellow prisoners. Once out of jail, he founded an organization for ministering to prisoners and promoting prison reform. He wrote books—first about his own life, then expressing his deep concerns about life in his country and in his world.

Many years have passed since that night in 1973 when Chuck Colson experienced his personal "earthquake." At this stage we can safely call the change both real and lasting. Whether the change is for the better depends perhaps on your point of view. But Chuck Colson believes that the process of change which began that August night was a change that brought reality to his life, a reality that has proven infinitely more satisfying than he could ever have anticipated.

THREE

Coming to Ourselves: Facing Up to Reality

It is just as it was when you passed it before, but your eyes are altered. You see nothing now but realities.

C.S. Lewis

Humankind cannot bear very much reality.

T.S. Eliot

ONE OF THE CLASSIC STORIES of human change is found in the New Testament—the story of the Prodigal Son. Actually, I believe that title is a poor one, because the central figure in the story is actually the father rather than the son who left him. Still, the son's part of the story is a vivid portrait of what happens in the inner earthquake called repentance.

You probably know the story (see Lk 15:11-32). The so-called prodigal son was a young man who claimed his share of the inheritance his father would eventually have left to him and his brother. He then left the country in pursuit of glamour and fun. The foolish young man quickly spent his small fortune, was forsaken by his friends, and finally got a job as a swineherd. This job which Jews hated and despised paid so poorly that he found himself hungrily eyeing the pig's food. To compound his difficulties, the country was in the midst of a depression and the threat of disease.

Finally, he came to his senses. He admitted to himself that his father's servants were better off. He had not only been a fool, but also a scoundrel in the way he had treated his father. The more he thought about it, the worse he felt. Perhaps for the first time, he somehow realized that he was utterly unworthy of the love his father had shown him.

At last he made up his mind. "I will set out and go back to my father and say to him: 'Father, I have sinned against heaven and against you. I am no longer worthy to be called your son; make me like one of your hired men'" (Lk 15:21).

In that moment, the prodigal son began his journey home. For it was in that moment that he faced the reality of who he was and who he had become. The New Testament says "he came to himself," which is to say he began seeing himself and the world realistically.

The dominoes had set themselves up in the previous weeks as his money ran out, and as one by one his fairweather friends dropped him. Resentment, bitterness, self-disgust, and hatred began to haunt him in succession. Then, in a moment, his whole view of the world shifted. The inner revolution began, the dominoes tumbled, the earth moved—and suddenly nothing looked the same. "What a heel I'm being. And what a fool! I don't have to stay here. I will return to my father."

REPENTANCE: A NEW VIEW OF REALITY

What happened to the prodigal son also happened to Chuck Colson on his friend's front porch. Listening to a reading of C.S. Lewis, his view of things suddenly shifted and he saw himself as he really was: "Suddenly I felt naked and unclean, my bravado defenses gone. I was exposed, unprotected, for Lewis's words were describing me.... Just as a man about to die is supposed to see flash before him, sequence by sequence, the high points of his life, so as Tom's voice read on that August evening, key events in my life paraded before me."[1]

It happened to my friend Betty, too, when she finally faced the fact that when she drank she was a terrible mother, that she stopped caring. While attending AA, she admitted that she couldn't stop drinking without the help of "God as she understood him." It happened to Ward Gasque as he took a hard look at where his eating and exercise habits were taking him.

But here's the rub: a similar shift of vision happened to the students in the Chinese university who "repented" of being bourgeois. And it happened when Betty started to "hate God's guts." Hate and anger are uncomfortable feelings. At that point Betty began to drown her anger with alcohol.

All of these individuals, in their moment of repentance, underwent a major shift in viewpoint—what some people call a *paradigm shift*. They saw themselves in a different light, facing truths about themselves they may have denied earlier. Their view of reality changed, and subsequently their lives changed also.

Real and lasting change cannot take place without such a change in the way we see things. But the question naturally arises: If *all* repentance and change involves a changed view of reality, then what view of reality is involved in repentance that is positive and healthy? What kind of inner earthquake results in "good change?"

And the answer that suggests itself is both simple and profoundly mysterious: Positive repentance involves facing reality that is *real*.

This can get philosophically tricky, of course. Relativists (many psychologists among them) would say that *any* reality is valid if it's "real for you." But such a viewpoint robs us of any way of distinguishing between healthy and unhealthy repentance. I believe this is one reason psychology has proved limited in its ability to help people change. When we deny the existence of any fundamental reality that is greater than we are, any moral structure in the universe, we limit our ability to direct people toward positive and lasting transformation.

As I have said, I am a Christian. I am convinced that God is the central Reality of the universe and that the way to God is to be found in Jesus Christ. I also believe that the basic mechanism of lasting and positive change—the inner revolution or earthquake we have been talking about—is available to anyone. It is part of the way we were made.

I do not believe, however, that all inner revolutions are equally positive or healthy. My experience has shown me that repentance is positive *only* to the extent that it involves aligning oneself, to a greater or lesser extent, with the reality of the way the universe is made.

Reality is *not* subjective. There is a moral structure to the universe. The essence of positive and lasting change is aligning ourselves with that structure. And that means facing reality—about ourselves, about our environment, and hopefully about Reality itself.

WHY REALITY IS HARD TO FACE

Anyone who has lived in the world knows that facing reality is not easy. As Chuck, Betty, Ward, and the prodigal son discovered, coming to terms with the way things are is painful—sometimes very painful.

But why is reality hard to face—so hard, in fact, that it often takes an inner revolution to help us see it?

One reason is that reality presents us at times with mutually exclusive choices. I remember seeing two men on the island of Trinidad who were setting a monkey snare. They made a hole in a coconut shell just large enough to fit a monkey's paw. They then tied the shell to a tree, and half filled it with peanuts. Eventually a monkey fell for the bait, only to find that while it was able to insert an empty paw, it could not withdraw a fistful of nuts. Either it would have to release the nuts or remain stuck in the cocunut shell.

The lure of the food was compelling. Refusing to admit defeat, the little creature continued to struggle for both nuts *and* freedom—an impossibility. It grew frantic as its captors approached, but seemed unable to release the nuts. The monkey was taken away captive—and without the nuts.

Life often confronts us with mutually exclusive choices. To simultaneously embrace two incompatible desires can lead to pain and tragedy. To choose freedom involves facing the pain of doing without the peanuts.

But a more basic reason underlies the pain of facing reality: in the depth of our being—whatever we may protest to the contrary—all of us have an insatiable craving to be loved. And we have a deep-down fear that we won't be.

Love is essential to all higher life forms. The higher the life form, the more necessary love becomes to physical survival. Without love we begin, quite literally, to die. For this reason, all of us harbor a terrible fear of rejection. We may be unaware of this craving for love and fear of rejection. They may be buried deep in our unconscious minds. Yet subtly and powerfully, these feelings influence our behavior and distort our view of life around us.

This deep and insatiable need for love and the consequent fear of rejection lie at the root of our difficulty in facing reality, as well as our difficulty in changing. There are things about ourselves and the people in our lives that we dare not face, because at a deep level we are desperately afraid that reality involves not getting the love we need.

The severity of our need to be loved has its roots in our early development. The earliest events in our lives are crucial. Being loved inadequately likely produces damage throughout our development, certainly well into our adolescent years. And the earliest damage is the most dangerous.

Many years ago, a psychoanalyst named René Spitz became puzzled about events in the orphanage for which he was responsible. A certain percentage of the tiny infants failed to thrive. They lost weight, stared listlessly, refused to nurse. Their faces looked dejected, their movements were slow, their development was retarded. Eventually these babies would lapse into a coma and die. He referred to the condition as *anaclitic depression*.[2] Spitz refused to accept this situation and set out to find a way to save the babies. He discovered that usually one of the nurses would be able to elicit some response from the infant, could awaken the child's attention. Different nurses could "connect with" different infants in this way. Spitz persuaded the staff that any nurses who could elicit a response from a dying infant should spend all their time with those particular babies— talking to them, carrying them in their arms, attempting to get them to nurse.

The scheme worked. Infants who were thus allowed to "connect" with a specific nurse would grow more alert, put on weight, regain losses in their development. They would relate to the nurse as a mother. Spitz concluded that the infants had been dying of grief over the loss of their mothers— the loss of love.

But what is love to a newborn infant? How does the infant understand love? What specifically were the little orphans missing that the nurse was able to provide? Was it her smell? Her voice? The feel of her arms? The sight of her breast and the feel of the nipple to the child's lips? In what did the love consist?

In seeking to answer these questions, Sigmund Freud and other early psychoanalysts focused on the breast and the mother's nipple, the source of life-giving nourishment. This now seems much less important than Freud thought. In 1958 Harry Harlow threw a great deal of doubt on Freud's view by describing a remarkable series of experiments with infant monkeys.

Harlow had noticed that infant monkeys fed from sterile

bottles survived better in captivity than those breast-fed by their mothers. However they became deeply attached to pads of soft gauze diaper, spending more time clinging to the pads than to any cuddly toy. The baby monkeys seemed to treat the diaper material in the same way human young-sters cling to "security blankets."

Intrigued, Harlow and his wife took eight infant monkeys from their mothers and placed them in identical cages with a choice of two mechanical surrogate "mothers" in each, plus the pad of diaper gauze. Both mothers had crude wooden heads, painted to represent a monkey's face. Both had cylin-drical wire-mesh bodies. The only difference between them was that one wire mesh body was wrapped in soft terrycloth toweling, while the other had a "body" of bare wire. In four of the cases, a nipple protruded from a feeding bottle inside the bare wire-mesh mothers, and in the others from within the terry towel mothers. Thus four monkeys could nurse from an uncomfortable sort of mother, and the other four could feed from a soft and cuddly mother.

Both groups fed well and gained weight equally. But all eight spent much more time clinging to the terry towel mother. The four who were fed by the bare wire mother only went to her to feed. All eight, when startled, would fly to the terry cloth mother and cling to her. None of the eight became attached to the pads of soft diaper gauze on the floor of the cage, and Harlow had them removed.[3]

Clearly, body contact with something soft provides little rhesus monkeys with the security of knowing someone loves them. Spitz's experiences in the orphanage indicate physical contact may be the key indication of love for little humans as well. There is growing evidence that this is true—and that physical contact remains critical during at least the first fif-teen years or so of our development. At a very basic level, we interpret the presence or absence of love according to comforting tactile sensations.

Add to this some other basic facts about life and human

development—that parents are imperfect, that the world is imperfect, and that children are apt to misinterpret the events that happen to them—and we begin to see how the deep-seated distortions in our view of reality begin. Children do not understand adults; they can misinterpret the kindliest of actions. This means they can be damaged not only by abuse and cruelty, but by good parenting as well.

There are many reasons, for instance, why a child might be denied the physical comfort he or she craves—and not all of them indicate a lack of love. A mother might become ill— or distracted and worried. Parents may be warned against "spoiling" a child. Another child in the family may be in a crisis and demand the lion's share of the parents' attention. For the child, however, all these conditions might easily be interpreted as lack of love. Rejection can be perceived—or misperceived—throughout childhood.

What does all this mean? Simply that all of us stand a good chance of growing up with a distorted view of reality. And that skewed sense of what is true about ourselves, about others, and about the universe leads us to make unhealthy, even dangerous choices about our lives. We become so entrenched in our misapprehended worlds that it really does take an earthquake to turn us around and get our vision straight.

HOW I LEARNED TO FACE MY OWN REALITY

Looking back at my own life from the perspective of maturity, I can now see my own parents more clearly than when I was a child. They were not bad parents; indeed I would rate them well above average. I am aware of their failures and weaknesses, but I also remember their many strengths.

And yet I have a distinct memory that changed the pattern of my understanding—both of myself and my world— for over fifty years. I describe my experience in part to show that a child's inability to read his parents' minds can damage that child just as surely as the vilest cruelties. But also I want to show the importance and power of repentance to reorder our distorted sense of reality.

The memory of that day is incomplete, much of it still inaccessible to me, locked deep in my unconscious mind. I see myself as a child of two, perhaps three. I am sitting on the floor, alone in a locked room for what seems like hours. I have been sobbing for a long while, but there is no use sobbing any more. I see myself in the aftermath of a child's sobbing—catching my breath in quick involuntary spasms from time to time. Probably I am being punished for something, but if so, it is the only time a locked room has been involved.

For the first time in my life, I know the despair that only a child can know. It is absolute despair, a final discovery of what the world is all about. I am accepting the fact that you never ask big people for kindness or understanding. You don't ask them for *anything*. It is an absolute sort of knowing, a rock-hard unchangeable knowing.

I understand clearly now that I must never again expect anything from any big person—and I silently vow never to do so. I could not articulate the vow, but it registered itself in the silence of my soul. And a child's vow, like a child's despair, must not be dismissed lightly.

That memory eluded me for many years. I still don't know why I was there, what had led to my confinement. I only know—and know very clearly—the terrible mood that gripped me, changing the course of my life.

Later I discovered that this event had made it impossible for me ever to accept affection and love from anyone. I could *give* affection. But all I expected in return was reasonable decency; I could not handle more than that. Over a forty-year period, I slowly came to understand that I was actually terrified of love and tenderness. As a child I had discovered how deceptive was the delusional hope of love. And I could not unlearn that lesson.

I grew up to be a "nice" person—indeed, "a very nice" person—but, because of my fear of love, a person you could never really get close to. I married, had five children, was successful in all I undertook. My fear of love, of which I was only vaguely aware in the early years, was not a fear of sexuality or of women. But I could not stand tenderness being shown toward me, even by my wife. Tenderness terrified me. I would react strangely to it, not understanding why.

Then one day I found myself face to face with my horror—the reality about myself—and that moment of confrontation changed my life. It was a Sunday, the fourth anniversary of my father's death. I was forty-four years old. All day I had felt mournful and depressed. In the evening, being a good evangelical Christian, I was praying with a couple of friends.

I had never believed in visions. Indeed, as a professor of psychiatry, I had regarded them as a sign of psychosis. And yet, as we kneeled together that evening, I suddenly became aware of something else in the room. About four feet in front of me and two feet above my eye level, a pair of bleeding, nail-pierced hands were extended to me from white sleeves. They were smooth, almost effeminate hands, such as a medieval artist might have painted of Christ. But I was not viewing a painting. The hands were three dimensional and solid, obscuring my view of the wall beyond.

I knew they were not the literal hands of Christ, but a sort of projection from my own brain. Yet I felt powerless before them. Heat went through my body. I wept helplessly. I trembled, sweated, was near to collapse. And I knew with a certainty that God was there. And strangely, I knew the hands had been there, extended to me, all my life, and that I had never noticed them before.

The hands were a silent invitation, saying, "Come, take hold of us!" They were love and friendship extended to me, friendship extended at the cost of blood. But my arms were paralyzed. I could no more raise them and take the proffered hands than I could fly. I sobbed piteously, begging God to break the psychological barriers with which I had surrounded myself in my fear of love.

All my life I had been refusing God's love for me, grieving him in the process. And I was powerless to change. I was sinning, and I could not stop. And here he was (and this was the most terrible of all), offering me love that cost him his life's blood. I wept in deepest, broken repentance.

As I write I am in my sixty-sixth year. Over the years since that night, the barriers I had erected against love have been gradually lowered. During the last three years, I have experienced a rapid acceleration in this process.

I was talking on the telephone the other day with a woman who knows me well. She asked me, "John, do you realize how much you have changed, especially during the last twelve months? You're transformed. You're a totally different person—free, open, vulnerable. You were never like this before!"

The change was made possible by an inner earthquake that began more than twenty years ago.

Yes, I have changed—and changed profoundly. Change can even happen to an old man. But my change is a proof of nothing, save the existence of a basic human mechanism that provides for radical change.

Psychologists could give a clear explanation of my vision. It does not prove the existence of God, nor do I include it with such a purpose. My belief in a loving God is based on a firmer foundation than having a vision. I believe it *was* God in this instance, but that is not my point.

No, I include the account as a somewhat dramatic illustration of the general principle that early events, early vows, early misinterpretations of reality can make us blind to our own essential problems, and lead us to misinterpret the nature of life itself.

All my life, I had misperceived authority figures, having an exaggerated sense of their importance. All my life, I had been unable to ask favors of anyone. I had wasted huge amounts of energy mending imaginary damaged fences. I had been unnecessarily guarded to friendly approaches, hiding in a defensive aloofness. *I had been living with a distorted view of reality.* Repentance has been changing me ever since.

To the extent that I distorted reality, I had been insane—for insanity is to live in unreality. My insanity did not prevent me from functioning, but it impaired my ability to function and robbed my relationships with others of the richness they might otherwise have had. I had inhabited a shrunken world, fearful of life's most precious gift—love. And I was too skilled in my performance—one so habitual that I did not realize it was a performance—to deceive all but the most acute observers.

WHAT WE DARE NOT SEE

If "good" parents can produce a distorted view of reality in their children, bad parents can do far greater harm. Even the moral strengths of a child can be seriously undermined and crippled by pathological parents. When parents batter a child, for instance, that child stands every chance of battering his or her children later, in spite of deep desires to the contrary. Similarly, a child who is the victim of sexual abuse may later abuse children sexually.[4] A child who loses a parent early in life has a greater chance of later depression.[5] And so I could go on. In all cases, early rejection or perceived rejection leads to distorted, unrealistic thinking.

You may say, "But I had a bad childhood, and I still think logically and see myself objectively." Unfortunately, it doesn't work that way. We would all like to believe our feelings do not limit our ability to be logical. They do, and to a far greater extent than we realize. Our perceptive processes distort much of what we see and hear.

Feelings are part of the raw material of logic; they affect

our thinking before its products even reach awareness. They form "filters" that keep us from hearing other people accurately.

Unfortunately, few of us—I would venture to say none of us—have received enough warm, soft cuddling in infancy. All of us also knew, or else falsely perceived, the threat of rejection in early childhood. Because of this, all of us face our adult lives with inadequate armor against the fear of being rejected by people around us. Fear shapes our behavior constantly, without our having any awareness of the fact.

Perhaps now we can dimly begin to see why so much pain accompanies change. To change, you have to face the fact that something about you is undesirable. The unexpressed question that goes with such awareness is, "What would they (or he or she) think if they knew?" So great is your fear of rejection that you rarely allow the question to surface. You bury your awareness of many undesirable traits in your unconscious mind.

All of us do it. And we go on doing so all our lives. We hide our undesirable traits in social situations and excuse those we cannot cover. Facing our buried negative traits means seeing ourselves as less loveable than we had thought. And that kind of awareness brings fear—fear that no one will love us, that we will be alone and rejected.

WHY HEALING OF MEMORIES ISN'T ENOUGH

All this would indicate that the cure for our distorted views of reality is relatively simple. If all our problems grow out of early misperceptions, all that should be necessary for healing is to uncover, understand, and correct the misconceptions.

This in essence was the approach taken by the early psychoanalysts. Freud and his followers correctly perceived that the roots of many of our difficulties lie buried in our unconscious minds. I believe, however, that Freud underestimated the problem. He and many of his followers felt that merely discovering and facing the buried pain would produce a return to normal behavior. And very occasionally this did happen. More commonly, however, patients undergoing psychoanalysis did not change any more profoundly than people who received no help, except in that they learned to discuss their problems in Freudian psychoanalytic jargon.

I believe the failure to effect real change lay in a failure to acknowledge that the universe has a moral structure—that guilt, shame, and fear are more than just projections of our minds. From childhood, we are responsible for our actions and our attitudes, even those that arise from misconceptions or mistreatment.

I mention this because some people pursue what is called *healing of memories* or *inner healing*, which has its roots in early psychoanalytic teaching. In this process of inner healing, a memory from earlier life is rediscovered from its hiding place in the unconscious mind. The idea is that the recovery of the memory, along with some comforting association (such as a mental picture of Jesus), will produce healing. Yet unless the moral aspects of the problem—which include the *response* of the person doing the remembering—are faced, the experience is unlikely to lead to permanent change.

Mary, let us say, has a homosexual orientation and hates being the way she is. As we work together, she recovers a long-forgotten memory of a terrible incident involving her parents, an incident that led to estrangement between Mary and her mother. Mary has often wondered about her difficulty in feeling close to her mother. She sobs at the awfulness of what she is seeing through the eyes of her three-year-old self. The recovery of the memory opens the way to the recovery of her sense of normal womanhood.[6]

There is more to the story, however, than the memory of the wrong done by the parent. Also involved is an ongoing wrong attitude on Mary's part. For her childish bitterness has come an entrenched attitude of resentment—buried out of reach of her memory, but modifying her whole behavior. In order to be healed, therefore, Mary has to face the reality about what she has become, as well as the memory of what has happened to her. She has to give forgiveness and to *experience* forgiveness. And this will involve a radical realignment of her point of view—an earthquake, an inner revolution.

You can pursue the healing of memories in vain if this principle is ignored. It is repentance that makes the difference. I have known people to have endless "prayer sessions" as they chase more and more supposed roots of their difficulties—when all along their hearts have remained unrepentant and proud.

Author Jim McFadden tells the story of a man in his mid-thirties who had been cool and aloof toward his parents for some fifteen years. Both father and mother had been forced to work to support their family, which left little time to devote to personal attention and affection. The man asked for healing prayer for the deep sense of rejection he carried.

His main agenda was to get free from the pain he felt from his parents' neglect. I directed him to express forgiveness toward his mother and father, and to repent of his bitterness. He began, a bit grudgingly, to forgive them for a long list of grievances he had stored up in his heart.

Suddenly the Spirit of God moved on him in power. He burst into tears, abandoned his list of hurts, and began to sob out repentance for his sins against his parents. He had begun in high school by staying away from home as much as possible. When he graduated, he immediately took another job in town to put distance between himself and his folks. Under the conviction of the Holy Spirit he now saw how he had refused his parents the help they needed to care for the family. For the first time he saw clearly their dedication and unselfish love in the face of a great economic hardship. His hidden desire to punish was replaced by an earnest desire for reconciliation.[7]

THE NATURE OF INSANITY

Earlier I stated that my failure to perceive reality meant that I had been seeing the world through insane eyes. I also stated that I had been able to function fairly well even in my state of unreality. I was psychologically unhealthy; indeed, I would say I was psychotic. However, most people would have said I was functioning well.

I believe the definitions of psychosis provided by psychiatry andpsychology are seriously defective. Few of us live in touch with reality. But as long as we can cope with one another, sharing similar delusions or finding other people's delusions understandable, we assume we are all sane. Only the dysfunctionally insane are so labeled.

And what makes us dysfunctionally insane? We become dysfunctional when we cannot care for ourselves, when we become a danger to ourselves or to people around us. Few of us are dysfunctional in that sense. But most, perhaps all of us, are insane in the sense that we live in denial of reality.

I remember one of the first mental patients I encountered, a woman who for years had suffered from the terrible affliction of schizophrenia. Certainly she was out of touch with reality, but she was basically functional. That is, she could live at home, look after herself, and not upset other people.

Bertha became "insane" in the minds of the police on the morning she discovered her parents dead in bed. The elderly couple had made a suicide pact and died of an overdose of sleeping pills. Bertha knew her parents were dead, yet she was out of touch with the force of that reality. Following the discovery, she functioned with cold and terrifying efficiency, trivializing death.

"How did you feel? What did you do when you found

them?" her treating psychiatrist asked.

"Well, I called the dentist straight away."

"The *dentist*?"

"Yes, they couldn't attend their appointment if they were dead, could they?"

There was a terrible absence of emotional expression about the way she said it—a cold and frighteningly mechanical tone. She seemed to imply that we would certainly do the same ourselves. We can understand why the police shipped Bertha off to a mental institution.

Yet in our own way we may be just as out of touch with reality ourselves. But because we continue to function in a society of people who are also out of touch, we flatter ourselves we are sane. Our distortions differ—some of us are skewed one way, some another. But all of us, in our terror of rejecting and losing love, live lives of unreality.

MAPS TO NAVIGATE THROUGH LIFE

In describing our universal tendency to see the world insanely, psychiatrist and author Scott Peck says we create faulty "maps" of reality. The maps contain our basic understanding of reality which we use to navigate through life.

According to Peck, we create our maps through our contacts with other people, books, the media, and by interacting with reality. Our sources are all in some measure distorted, and our perception of them is likewise distorted. From the outset we ourselves have played fast and loose with truth, selecting what we have recorded on our maps. We therefore need to correct our maps year by year, as we face the truth about ourselves and the world around us.

This ongoing process of facing reality is the only way to be free, but it's not easy. As Peck puts it, "The process of making revisions is painful, sometimes excruciatingly painful."[8] As a result, many of us grow tired of the pain of updating our map. We give up our quest for understanding and content ourselves merely with owning our own map.

Some people give up in their teens and remain content with an adolescent view of life. Others hang on to middle age: "Their maps are small and sketchy, their views of the world narrow and misleading. By the end of middle age most people have given up the effort. They feel certain that their maps are complete and their Weltanschauung is correct (indeed even sacrosanct), and they are no longer interested in new information."[9]

Once this happens, we tend to get defensive about our maps. Should anyone challenge their accuracy, we become disturbed. Arguments about reality which challenge our view of life make us afraid. "We may denounce... new information as false, dangerous, heretical, the work of the devil. We may actually crusade against it, and even attempt to manipulate the world so as to make it conform to our view of reality.[10]

What Peck asserts is in some degree true of all of us, whatever our background, race, or creed. Because we are human, our hold on reality is flimsy. We know far less about ourselves than we think. Yet because our maps are the only key to reality we have, we cling to them with pitiful desperation—and still refuse to learn.

Perhaps that is why it so often takes an earthquake to persuade us to "come to ourselves"—to revise our maps, to take a good look at the pigsty we're living in, and to make that important first step on the road toward home.

POSITIVE CHANGE AND THE FEAR OF RELIGION

This is a book about change. Change that is profound and permanent can only come through the inner earthquake of repentance, and repentance has to do with the moral quality of reality. If I need to be changed, then I myself am in the wrong about something. I have wronged someone, and something must be done to rectify that wrong. The change must involve more than psychology.

If the change exists at a psychological level only—a sorting out of a problem that has its roots in my childhood—then it will rarely go deep enough to effect profound change. Unless I am, as it were, *made right with the basic structure of this universe of which I am a part*, the change is incomplete.

Here again, fear of rejection must be faced. Nonreligious people sometimes feel that religious people use God as a kind of emotional crutch. To some extent they are correct. Many people who claim to be Christians have created their own God, giving him benign and comforting features that differ from his true face. God can be a terrifying reality. So if the idea of God scares you, you can always repaint his face.

The mechanism works both ways. Both religious and nonreligious people modify their ideas of a supreme being because of their fears of rejection. If some people use God as a crutch, others avoid the idea of God out of unconscious fear—the terrible fear of ultimate rejection. If rejection by another human being is terrifying, what shall we say about rejection by Someone who owns us and truly knows us—who is the ultimate source of all existence? Better to pretend there is no such person.

Psychiatrists and psychologists sometimes play mind games on this theme. My own psychiatric teachers—who knew about my missionary past—were so outwardly confident in their antireligious posture that they put money into a pool. The winner would be the person who guessed most closely when I would renounce my Christian beliefs.

I didn't know about the pool until much later, so I was a little puzzled when one after another my psychiatric teachers would ask me, "John, what can it have been in your childhood that caused you to need the comfort of a God?"

Nevertheless, I soon found that a good offense was the best defense. "I'm wondering the same about you," I would reply. "What could it have been in *your* infancy that makes you so scared of God?"

"But I'm not scared!"

"Aha! Now you're going into denial! If you're not scared, why is it you can never get away from the subject? How come you always bring it up?" Ten years passed before I learned about the bet. I never did discover what happened to the money. But I'm convinced the questions I asked my teachers were valid ones.

I cannot prove the existence of God either by argument or by science, so I will not try to do so in this book. I am convinced these change mechanisms can apply to anyone— Christian or non-Christian. Of course I believe that the deepest, most redemptive change flows from coming to terms with what God has done through Christ.

But regardless of one's specific religious stance, the basic psychological truth holds: we are all afraid of reality. But no one ever really changes for the better without somehow facing up to the truth.

FOUR

The Beast in the Basement: Evil and Reality

The world is still deceived with ornament.
In law, what plea so tainted and corrupt
But, being seasoned with a gracious voice,
Obscures the show of evil? **William Shakespeare**

For what I do is not the good I want to do; no, the evil I do not want to do—this I keep on doing. **St. Paul [Romans 7:15]**

O UR LAST CHAPTER BEGAN by recognizing that repentance is in essence a shift in point of view, a facing of and response to reality. It also stressed that reality is not subjective—that the universe has a moral structure, and that the essence of positive change is aligning oneself with that moral structure. But there's a dark side of reality, or rather a negative counterfeit. Traditionally, this big lie about reality is called evil.

Evil has long been a subject of debate among philosophers and religious thinkers. Certain streams of thought have declared that evil is only imaginary or easily conquered by the use of reason. Others have held that evil is not to be fought, but simply accepted as coequal with good. This belief is accepted unthinkingly by large sections of the world's population. Oriental mysticism and New Age teachings are based on the doctrine that evil is a part of life, even of the divine nature, and that darkness will forever be equal to light. The influential psychoanalyst Carl Jung believed this, portraying God as a combination of good and evil.[1]

Beyond the philosophical debates, however, we must deal with human actions and decisions. Here on this basic level, evil is hard to deny and even harder to accept. Evil vaunts its proud hatred in religion, in politics, in every aspect of life. We have only to think of racial hatred and violence, or of the abuse and abandonment of children, or of the blind greed of many large corporations to know that evil must be fought wherever it appears.

Evil on this planet typically has to do with "man's inhumanity to man." This reality reveals itself in cruelty, exploitation of the weak, racism, violence, and sexual exploitation in families. It manifests itself primarily in the disruption of the relationships we have with one another as human beings. Evil cannot be tolerated. But can it be overcome? That question rests at the heart of the issue of change.

THE EVIL IN ALL OF US

Woody Allen's superb film, *Crimes and Misdemeanors*, takes a very serious look at evil, and seems to conclude that there is no moral structure to the universe. If there were, Allen asks, how could we explain all the evil the world has experienced just in the last century—the Holocaust, the Khmer Rouge, Idi Amin?

How explain it? Evil is part of the reality of who we are. It exists in us all because we—the entire human race—have chosen to run our lives our own way. If we believe we have evil under control, then we have never seriously tried to be rid of it.

Twenty centuries ago, St. Paul gave us the classic account of what happens to a person who seriously purposes to live a good life. Most of us do not pursue evil, but neither do we commit ourselves to leading model lives. We aim at "passing grades"—whatever society tolerates and whatever else we can get away with. Any serious commitment to live a truly good life can cause us serious problems, for then we are confronted with the sobering reality of the evil within us. Paul describes what happened to him:

> I do not understand what I do. For what I want to do I do not do, but what I hate I do.… For I have the desire to do what is good, but I cannot carry it out. For what I do is not the good I want to do; no, the evil I do not want to do—this I keep on doing.… So I find this law at work: When I want to do good, evil is right there with me. For in my inner being I delight in God's law; but I see another law at work in the members of my body waging war against the law of my mind and making me a prisoner of the law of sin at work within my members. What a wretched man I am! Who will deliver me from this body of death?
>
> **(Rom 7:15-24, NIV)**

Not all of us discover this, because we do not seriously aim high. We never discover what I would call *the beast in the basement,*—a beast that lurks in all of us, although we are but rarely aware of its existence.

Most of us, of course, never "side with evil" in its more blatant forms. We are "nice" people, and as such we are blind to the virulence of evil in all of us. In normal times, and in most levels of society, it is easy to ignore the reality of evil and become complacent about it. In times of crisis, however, we can see more clearly the destructive work of evil.

Long before his fame as the Watergate prosecutor, Leon Jaworski discovered in Germany the terrible reality of evil that lurks in ordinary people. His education began as he investigated the murder of a German by his fellow captives in a prisoner of war camp.

A suspected ringleader, a pastor named Ludwig, was an ardent Nazi. A search of the pastor's quarters turned up a hidden diary, which Jaworski examined. He writes,

> I was shocked by his gloating satisfaction when a fellow prisoner was beaten bloody for his failure to adhere to the Nazi line. "They were supposed to be taken care of [killed], but the Americans rescued them in time. But first we really beat them until they were bleeding... "
>
> He went on to detail the victim's suffering and seemed quite pleased that "the defectors" were being punished so well. The more the blood and gore, the better he appeared to like it. As I read on, the diary became a filthy thing and I wanted to wash my hands after handling it.[2]

How could a pastor gloat over bloody beatings? Do we label Ludwig a hypocrite? Do we make sage comments about his sexuality and his unconscious psychological conflicts? Or do we face the fact that everyone, even religious leaders, contain the capacity for great cruelty? (In fact, people with the greatest potential for goodness, even holiness, have by the same token a great potential for diabolical evil. The greater our capacity, it seems, the greater our potential either to be saints or devils.)

Jaworski's education had only begun. Later, as the Chief Prosecutor at the Nazi War Crimes Trials in Nuremburg, he saw the lesson even more clearly. The incident under review had occurred in the sleepy little German town of Russelsheim.

Because of damaged railway lines, a group of downed American fliers bound for prison camp had to be marched a short distance through the town. A crowd gathered to watch them. A few members of the crowd hurled rocks. The aggression gathered momentum into an orgy of killing as the airmen were mobbed and mercilessly beaten to death.

Men and women alike took part in the bloodletting. The prisoners' guards either could not or would not protect them. Appeals by concerned church members to their clergy went unheeded; both Catholic priest and Protestant pastor were afraid to intervene.

"Finally, two hours later, all of the airmen [lay] in pools of blood, most of them now shapeless masses of blood and bone.... As I thought of Joseph Hartgen, the two sisters, and the other 'good-hearted' townspeople of Russelsheim, I realized that none of us know what we are capable of doing until we reach such a point. As we cannot envision the heights we can reach by placing ourselves in the hands of God, neither can we imagine the depths to which we can sink without him."[3]

Not long ago I watched a TV documentary produced by a young Jewish Canadian woman, the daughter of an Auschwitz survivor. She was struggling to come to terms with what had happened to her parents and grandparents, to understand how it could have happened. As part of the program, she interviewed the granddaughter of the vice-commandant of Auschwitz. When asked if she could understand what happened in Nazi Germany, the woman shook her head no. She remembered her grandfather as a kindly man who enjoyed his grandchildren and had been very loving to them. Was it possible, she wondered, that such persons had two souls?

Perpetrators of such crimes do not have two souls. Neither are foul deeds the product of a particular "type" of person. Jews and Germans alike are capable of committing heinous acts of evil. So are Americans, Canadians, British people, Chinese people—whoever. The more recent butcheries in Tiananmen Square and in Rumania in 1989 and

1990 were not the acts of monsters, but of affectionate parents and grandparents.

All such atrocities have to do with something that exists deep in our own personalities. Once let loose in a social group, or in a nation, there is no limit to the evil. All of us are potential mass murderers.

HOW EVIL ERUPTS

If all of us have the potential for horrific evil, why does evil so often seem contained? What conditions cause it to break out in all its virulence?

Social conditions and even intellectual atmosphere play an important part, as demonstrated in the advent of Nazi Germany. In the Wiemar Republic, after World War I, ideas and lifestyles emerged that paved the way for Auschwitz and Dachau. Disillusioned and humiliated after World War I, Germans of that era escaped into hedonism. As Malcolm Muggeridge writes,

> All the most horrible and disgusting aspects of the last decades of the twentieth century—the pornography, the sadism, the violence, the moral and spiritual vacuum—were already in evidence there.

> In this sick environment, the notion of mercy-killing was put forward in 1920 in a book entitled *The Release and Destruction of Life Devoid of Value*, by Alfred Hoche, a reputable psychiatrist, and Karl Binding, a jurist. The authors advocated killing off "absolutely worthless human beings," pointing out that the money spent on keeping them alive could be used... on helping a young married couple set up house.... The Hoche-Binding book... crystallized the thinking of a whole generation.[4]

These ideas and attitudes, in turn, gradually led to the

evils of the Holocaust. Dr. Leo Alexander, who worked with Leon Jaworski at the Nuremburg Tribunal, comments:

> Whatever proportion these crimes finally assumed, it became evident to all who investigated them that they had started from small beginnings... merely a subtle shift in the attitude of physicians. It started with the acceptance of the attitude... *that there is such a thing as life not worthy to be lived* [my italics].... Gradually the sphere of those to be included in this category was enlarged to encompass the socially unproductive, the ideologically unwanted, the racially unwanted, and finally all non-Germans.[5]

Ironically, within thirty brief years the same philosophies that culminated in the Nuremburg trials had gained currency in the very nations that sponsored the Nuremburg condemnation of the Holocaust. "Let us," we began to say, "let us abolish unwanted life! Let us become the arbiters of life and death." Muggeridge muses on the irony that 1979, the Year of the Child, saw fifty million abortions performed. We who decry the horrors of the Holocaust are not immune to the thinking that caused it!

Evil at its most virulent, therefore, seems to be concentrated in certain social movements. Once again, however, the trends could never arise, much less gain momentum, if there were not a beast in every one of our basements. This is the only possible explanation of incidents such as that of Russelsheim, where respectable citizens embarked on a murderous orgy.

Because our own evil is mixed with good (and because, as we saw in the last chapter, the reality about ourselves is so hard to face), we tend to think we are "as good as the next person." The moment we embark on an evil course with others, however, we pool the evil inside each of us. Then evil becomes a social power. Even if we avoid taking part, it may be because we sense the evil within us and turn away in terror.

Giving the beast even a little freedom is a risky game. It can rapidly gain power in the form of a lynching mob, or a riot, or even a war.

LAW AND THE RESTRAINT OF EVIL

In "good times," it is easy to assume that our own will or even our innate decency is responsible for keeping us "good." In actuality, laws and social structures are the boundaries that keep most of us out of trouble most of the time. When these structures break down, the beast emerges. That is one reason dictatorships tend to be evil. The rulers themselves may not be exceptionally evil, but the lack of legal restraints makes the evil in them freer to ripen.

Where legal restraints weaken or are thrown off by dictatorship, evil arrogantly prowls the streets. At such times, citizens live in fear. When law is weak in Colombia, good people dread cocaine barons. In Panama, when Noriega's bullies ruled the streets, good people stayed near home.

Without the restraint of law, evil can grow without limit, culminating in murder and the ultimate destruction of a society—chaos. Today, as law in the West grows progressively weaker, the power of evil increases daily. Our belief in individual freedom, therefore, must be tempered by a clear realization of the evil within all of us.

Of course, even when the rawer aspects of evil are contained by law, evil is not totally hidden. It emerges in more civilized forms: vicious gossip; professional manipulation; "everybody does it" forms of cheating. All of these give evidence of the beast within us. So do apathy in the face of suffering, indifference to need, the unwillingness to get involved in meeting needs. (It's no accident that the classic confessional prayer from *The Book of Common Prayer* asks forgiveness for "what we have done, and... what we have left undone.") Snobbishness, petty lusts, endemic selfishness, little lies and minor insults—all the jockeying we commonly do to keep ourselves on top and others underneath do their part to keep the beast alive. Then, in times of crisis, it emerges in all its terrifying power.

I first met the phenomenon of "the beast in the basement"—and understood the law's importance in controlling it—in a Bolivian leper colony as a member of the New Tribes Mission. Embarrassed by their inability to handle the colony's problems, the Bolivian government asked us to take care of it.

I was assigned the medical care of the patients. Gradually, I and my colleagues grew to know, respect, and to love these people. They learned to trust us, too. Most of the residents were ordinary people, the kind of people you would be happy to have as neighbors.

Once, however, when the director was away and my wife and I were alone in the colony, a fight broke out between two of the men. One man wounded the other in the head with his machete, then disappeared into the jungle. Why had he fled, I wondered? The wound was not that bad. What terror drove him into hiding?

As I sewed and bandaged the wounded man's head, I began to understand. As the men of the colony gathered round to watch, they seemed tense and restless. Isolated mutterings began to gather into an angry consensus: "We'll lynch him!"

When we came to the colony, we had heard ugly rumors of previous lynchings—grisly stories about bodies swinging from trees. But we had paid little attention to the rumors. Even if they were true, we had reasoned, our presence would end such practices. We had been naive.

The more the men of the colony talked, the darker grew the cloud of fear and hatred hovering over them. Their faces became masks of evil. The women in the colony stared at them in fearful silence. My private sympathies were with the aggressor, whom the wounded man had cheated out of his turn at the irrigation ditch.

Full of fear I turned to face the crowd of men and said, "You will have to lynch me before you will be free to lynch him. I will go with you wherever you go, and I will stop you with my life if I have to. We need to learn law here. However great the wrong, law is the answer, not lynching."

Curiously, the men of the colony seemed relieved and began to relax. We argued a lot as the tension subsided, but finally they allowed me to go in search of the aggressor. I was to be accompanied by no one but the fugitive's wife.

We soon found him, a pathetic young man cowering in his hiding place in the forest. It took us some time to convince him that we would and could protect him. But at last he agreed to accompany us and to face a just trial.

Once we were back I patiently—and it took a great deal of patience—taught the members of the colony a model of law based on my scant knowledge of the British legal system. We appointed a jury and examined witnesses. As self-appointed judge, I ran the trial. When the jury returned a guilty verdict, I decided what the sentence should be.

A very frightening situation had been resolved. In resolving it I had learned a big lesson, a lesson I never forgot. Murder and mob violence lie just beneath the surface of the human soul. Law may help contain it. Fear may unleash it. But neither makes it a whit less powerful. The beast in the basement is real.

THE UNREAL NATURE OF EVIL

But what exactly is evil?

The question is perplexing, and the definition difficult. It is even problematical to say that evil is *real*. Of course it is real, in the sense that it exists, that it must be faced and fought, that it has power.

In another sense, however, evil is the counterfeit of all that is real, a bad copy of the moral structure of the universe. Evil is not so much the equal opposite of good as its negative reflection.

Look at yourself in a mirror. Is what you see real? Evil bears the same relation to good as the "backward" image in the mirror bears to you. Your image does not stand a foot or two behind the mirror in the way you see it. It is created only from light rays reflected back to your eye. You are real. Your reflection is real only in the sense that it derives its existence from yours.

In the same way, evil derives its existence from reality. Goodness has a real existence, and would still shine out were all evil to be abolished. But if good were abolished, evil would disappear.

Evil is not just a derivative, however, but a distortion as well. It gives a false reflection of reality—just as fun-house mirrors make us look too large, or too small, or crooked. Evil is not only an "unreal" reflection of reality, but the "big lie" about reality.

Evil therefore gains its great power from our human acceptance of the lie. The more we believe in this unreal power, the greater its hold over us. It doesn't follow, however, that evil can be abolished simply by our ceasing to believe in it. (Christian Science has, I believe, taken this thought too far.)

Because evil is derivative, it can never ultimately triumph. Its victories are local and impermanent. Nevertheless, because this negative and distorted reflection is embedded so deeply in us, we cannot overcome it by a simple act of will. It is too much a part of us to be so easily overcome.

EVIL AND THE SUPERNATURAL

In Western society, evil has traditionally been personified as Satan, the fallen angel, God's enemy—and his followers. Evil was seen as a supernatural force coming from "the Father of Lies" and his followers.

That attitude has gradually changed in the past few centuries. Western society in general grew skeptical about anything that was supposed to reflect the supernatural. Science had shown that there was no such thing. We were no longer "superstitious."

Over the past few decades, although the "scientific" view still holds superficial sway, there has been a new openness to the idea of the supernatural—including supernatural evil. Media accounts involving ghosts, spirits, and reincarnation are no longer rare, even in respected publications. Newspaper accounts of crimes and trials sometimes hint at satanic rituals or ritual abuse.[6]

This rapid public swing toward acceptance of the supernatural undoubtedly reflects a great deal of superstition. The New Age movement is supernatural in its basic tenets and has had a strong influence in certain sectors. (I believe it is not nearly as benign as it claims to be.) But surely some part of this change can be attributed to the fact that dismissing or explaining away the supernatural doesn't make it *go* away.

In October 1985, a highly publicized trial involving a group of alleged Satan worshipers began in Canada and lasted eighteen months. Many similar trials had already taken place in the United States. This particular trial concerned ritual murder, cannibalism, and rituals in a remote burial ground—during which recently buried coffins were opened, and their contents added to. But its most sensational aspects involved the abuse of two little girls who were forced, among other things, to "eat poo" (human excrement).

I began to read a book describing this trial[7] while travelling on an airplane. I have had a lot of experience with the seamier side of life and am accustomed to foul smells, gore, blood, and corpses. Although the book did not represent sensationalist journalism, at one point, in sudden panic, I tore my seat belt open and rose to make a swift dive for the toilet, struggling not to vomit in the aisle. My deepest human instincts told me that the acts described in the book represented evil that is bigger than anything merely human.

Satanism by its very tenets trains children and adults to overcome their natural instincts and inhibitions. This is the reason for the eating of human excrement, the ritual murders and deception, the cruelty to children and to others we would naturally protect, the bizarre sexual practices. From the satanic perspective, strength and spiritual power lie in overcoming normal human instincts. Every last remnant of "human feeling" must be expunged, so that a person will be free to act in any way. Satanism aims at inculcating the big lie into the center of the human soul.

Witchcraft (even the "white," purportedly benign sort) and Satanism display the same derivative nature of all evil. For this reason, there are surface similarities between these evil systems and the Judeo-Christian tradition. Both hold strongly to belief in supernatural spirit beings. The miraculous is an essential component of both. Fundamental to both is the belief in the efficacy of sacrifice.

But at that point the comparison stops. Instead of the power of love, true witchcraft believes in its most extreme antithesis—the power of hate. In place of the power of truth, it places the power of the lie. And whereas the ultimate sacrifice in Christian tradition is the self-giving in personal sacrifice, that of Satanism is the sacrifice of helpless victims.

I personally believe in the existence of supernatural evil. Since I believe in God, the living Reality, then of necessity I am forced to believe in Satan, the distorted image of that reality. Since I believe that God is active in the world, I cannot help but believe in the active presence and power of Satan in the world.

But even if I did not believe in God, events such as those recounted in the Satanist trial, massive evil such as evidenced in the Holocaust, and even "everyday" varieties of cruelty and pride are enough to convince me that there is an evil bigger than we are.

THE ORIGINS OF EVIL—A CHRISTIAN VIEW

In one sense, evil is like a virus that has infected the whole of our planet. According to Christian theism, it existed elsewhere before it came here. Let me summarize the Christian view of evil's origins. I find that most people who criticize it have never understood it.

First, Christianity is founded on belief in a particular kind of God. The God who made everything is not a force, but a person. He has always existed, and he made everything out of nothing by his own power and genius. He is also present everywhere, but that is not to say that everything is part of him. He is distinct from what he created, even though he is present everywhere in it.

Far from being a blind force, God is even more of a person than you or I. Think of the progression from insect to dog to human being—not just in terms of size, but in complexity and personality. At one end you have something that functions like a machine, even though it has life. You would never treat it as a person—not unless you were writing a story for small children. A dog would represent a big leap forward in that progression. Sometimes we say, "That dog's almost human!" Extend the line further from dogs through human beings to God, and you may begin to understand what I mean by saying God is *more of* a person that we are. In whatever way we may define the essence of personhood, we find it more highly developed in God himself.

According to Christian teaching, this divine person is both a moral being and a perfect moral being. To be perfect, he must be loving. He is also all-powerful. These two facts raise the obvious question. If he is both loving and all-powerful, why do we have to suffer evil? Even more problematic, why is there evil in each one of us?

There are some things that even an all-powerful God cannot do. Certain propositions are by their nature *intrinsically* impossible. Even God cannot make a perfectly spherical cube. The concept is nonsensical, and God does not create nonsense. More importantly, God can choose to limit his power. He did in fact do so when he created us.

Because he made us for companionship with himself, God was not content merely to rule us. He wanted a love relationship. A person can only love when he or she is free to choose. Love that is a blind unreasoning instinct apparently was not what God was after. He wanted us to *choose to* love him. The words *android* and *humanoid* have been added to our vocabulary in the twentieth century, and now whole races of both evil and benign nonhuman beings populate movies and TV. Few serious thinkers expect that such things could love, hate, or be good companions. God did not create a race of "droids" to love and be loved by, but a race of persons.

But if the power of choice is to be involved in our personhood, then God must limit himself. And that means we can choose *not* to love him. We can choose to rebel against him, to "do our own thing." We can choose lies instead of reality. And early in the history of the human race, we chose to do just that. We discovered evil by tasting it. We opened Pandora's box, and once we had opened it, we had to live with the consequences.

Christian teachers have always proclaimed the existence of supernatural beings. The Bible goes further, telling us that evil was brought to our planet by Satan—a being who was created by God as an angel, but who rebelled against him. Christians and Jews alike debate about the literal truth of the story, and the debate may be important, but the meaning of the story is clear enough. It is meant to teach us that at the dawn of human history we made a choice, a choice to believe a lie about reality. In so doing, we gave evil its power. The Lord of Lies, Satan, began to rule over territory that had once belonged to God. Now Satan rules us because we as a species invited him here.

Since God respected his own image in us, he respected our choice. But he did not abandon us to destruction. Instead, he is perpetually seeking to win us back. Throughout history there have been men and women who were won back, serving as witnesses to truth. However, most of us now live under the power of the lie we believed, and under the power of its author.

In the Christian view, God has made a way back for us, but at a great personal cost. This reconciling act of God makes it possible for us to recognize evil and turn from it. It is the act of God that makes repentance possible.

THE MOMENTUM OF EVIL

Many observers have commented that there seems to be a progression of evil in human beings. Both "big evil" of Holocausts and Satanism and less obvious, personal evil seem to grow from relatively insignificant beginnings.

Robert Louis Stevenson pictured such a progression vividly in his classic story, *The Strange Case of Dr. Jekyll and Mr. Hyde.* As you may remember, Dr. Jekyll and Mr. Hyde are the same person. Jekyll is a doctor who pursues his chosen career with dedication and compassion. Like anyone, he is not perfect, and he has "sown his wild oats," but on the whole he has led a controlled, exemplary life.

One day, however, Dr. Jekyll discovers a chemical formula that will release the evil part of him, temporarily destroying his noble aspects and transforming him for a time into the diabolical residue that remains.

After Jekyll ingests the formula, his body actually shrinks several inches, and what is left is ugly and repulsive. However, he experiences a surge of energy and a fierce exultation. He tells a friend, "I knew myself to be more wicked, tenfold more wicked, sold a slave to my original evil; and the thought, in that moment, braced and delighted me like wine. I stretched out my hands, exulting in the freshness of these sensations.[8]

For Jekyll, indulging in evil is like credit card buying—have fun now, pay later. Drinking the formula gives Jekyll experiences in evil that he could never enjoy freely in his normal state. As Hyde, he can do what he cannot do as Jekyll. He begins to spend his nights as the one and his days as the other. Hyde's wickedness reaches the point that returning home one early morning, he collides with a small girl, knocks her down, and tramples her.

However, Jekyll still believes he can control the situation. He boasts to his lawyer who believes Hyde to be Jekyll's friend, "I tell you one thing, the moment I choose, I can be rid of Mr. Hyde."[9] Jekyll has deceived himself with a delusion we may all at times share.

Over time, however, something happens to Jekyll's ability to control his switches into Hyde. It grows progressively easier for him to become Hyde and harder to return to Jekyll. Jekyll writes in his confessions,

I began to spy a danger that, if this were much prolonged, the balance of my nature might be permanently overthrown, the power of voluntary change be forfeited, and the character of Edward Hyde become irrevocably mine.... Whereas, in the beginning, the difficulty had been to throw off the body of Jekyll, it had of late gradually but decidedly transferred itself to the other side.... To cast in my lot with Jekyll was to die to those appetites which I had long secretly indulged and had of late begun to pamper. To cast it in with Hyde was to die to a thousand aspirations.[10]

Jekyll's misgivings prove true. Hyde's activities become

wilder, and eventually he commits a murder. The story closes with Jekyll-Hyde's suicide.

Plants grow where conditions are favorable. The same is true of the evil in us. The more we indulge in evil, the more powerful the evil becomes. Eventually, we may reach the point where evil controls us.

Recently, I saw an example of the principle in a video made of Dr. James Dobson's interview with Ted Bundy, the notorious sex murderer. The interview took place a few hours before Bundy's execution. In the face of death, Bundy had dropped his con-artist persona. The reality and truthfulness with which he told Dobson his story was unmistakable.

Bundy's grim story began in a Christian home. Addiction to pornography led to a taste for the more exciting hard-core porn. This eventually gave rise to a controlling drive to live out his fantasies by committing sadistic sex murders on young women and children.

Evil indulged in eventually becomes evil that controls us. And that's not just true of mad scientists and serial murderers. It's a painful fact for many of us when we are forced to face the facts about ourselves.

THE ALLURE OF EVIL

But evil doesn't always *seem* ugly. In fact, the big lie of evil can be quite attractive.

Think about evil characters depicted in the media. Have you ever noticed how fascinating they tend to be? We are drawn to them with delicious shivers of horror.

I have always maintained that the less we know of evil, the better. Obviously we must know something about it in order not to be caught by it. To fear evil too greatly is to fall into the hands of evil. On the other hand, to be fascinated by evil is to be lured as the fabled bird into the jaws of the snake.

Make no mistake: evil does fascinate. I once wrote and published a fantasy for children about the battle between good and evil. The first cover design was done by a Japanese artist, who chose to portray good on the front of the book and evil on the back. The results were interesting. The front cover, the one depicting good, turned out sappy and sentimental. But the back cover, the one showing evil, was fascinating and gripping.

The artist herself commented that she found it much easier to portray evil than good. And she is not alone. In art, literature, films and videos, evil comes across as more exciting. It may repel us, but even that repulsion is somehow vivid and compelling. We look away, but almost immediately we want to look back again.

Evil almost seems more *alive*, even though in reality evil brings death. Villains have more sparkle, more chutzpah than saints. We relish them and envy their freedom to do the outrageous things they do. They challenge our sense of manhood or womanhood, making us feel somehow inferior.

Why is this? I can suggest a couple of reasons. I suppose evil fascinates us because it has already gotten its hooks into us. It is somehow entrenched in our deepest nature; we all have a beast in our basement. Something in us responds because evil is truly a part of us. Perhaps if we could root out the evil in ourselves, evil would lose its fascination.

Another reason evil fascinates us has to do with the inherent nature of evil. For evil has to do with lust—not just sexual lust, but any lust. A lust is a controlling desire for something "you just gotta have." Evil awakens the lust in us and draws us to it.

In *The Lion, the Witch and the Wardrobe*, C.S. Lewis has one of the four children in the story pass through a wardrobe in an old house, only to discover what his sister had previously discovered—that the wardrobe was a gateway to another world. Edmund then meets a wicked queen who asks him what he would like. Edmund chooses a candy called Turkish delight, so the queen conjures up a box containing several pounds of pleasure. Edmund has never tasted anything so delicious.

The queen knows that Edmund's brother and two sisters are aware of the wardrobe, and she wishes to lure them also into her power. The Turkish delight is her weapon, her means of control over Edmund. This enchanted delicacy, however, cannot really satisfy. "Anyone who had once tasted it would want more and more of it, and would even, if they were allowed, go on eating it till they killed themselves."[11] Edmund looks at the empty box, longing for more, but the queen will only give him more if he brings his brother and sisters to her.

In a sense, we, too, are under an enchantment. Evil has caught us in the same way the witch captured Edmund—by making us lustful. If we were honest with ourselves we could name the lusts which dominate our behavior. What we need is the key to every one of our lusts. It will have nothing to do (and yet everything to do) with sex and luxury and overeating. Evil fascinates us because it awakens a lust that cannot be satisfied.

PRIDE: THE SOCIALLY ACCEPTABLE EVIL

Still another reason we are so fascinated by evil relates to the very reason we as a race became involved with evil in the first place. According to the Bible, the key to our fall was pride. "You will be like God, knowing good and evil," the serpent told the woman, tempting her by appealing to her pride (Gen 3:5, NIV).

Ever since that day, we admire villains who lift their heads high, asserting their right to do and to have whatever they want. We watch them enviously—wishing, in our pride, that we were bold enough to copy them. Or we may even hold our own heads high and follow in their footsteps.

Curiously, pride is the very quality we try to inculcate into our children for their good. We define it, to be sure, as self-respect. "Nice girls don't do things like that." "Big boys don't cry." In other words we teach our children as we were taught ourselves—to overcome weaknesses and even vices by pride. As a result, we fail to see pride for the evil it is. Some of the most religious, the most upright and even "spiritual" people in the world are exceedingly proud people.

Yet pride makes us enemies of God. The Bible devotes little time to describing Satan, but one thing clearly stands out as his principle characteristic—pride. In the book of Proverbs we are told that "every one that is proud in heart is an abomination to the Lord (Prv 16:5, KJV)." Religious people? An abomination to God? Apparently so. The theme of God's hatred of religious pride continues all through the Bible.

Because pride is such a major element in evil, repentance often begins with the painful awareness of how great our pride is, which is precisely the way it began in Chuck Colson, if you remember. "The first step," says C. S. Lewis, "is to realize that one is proud. And a biggish step, too."[12]

There are two things about pride that we should know. The first is that it is often very hard to realize the extent of our own pride. "If you think you are not conceited," Lewis tells us, "it means you are very conceited indeed."[13] Other people's pride is easy to spot. Lewis explains that there is one vice "which everyone in the world loathes when he sees it in someone else.... And the more we have it ourselves, the more we dislike it in others."[14]

Do conceited people get under your skin, by any chance?

The second aspect of pride is even more serious: pride is the key to evil. At first, we might be inclined to dismiss the idea that pride is so very serious. After all, if "proper pride" can overcome vice, might it not also be good?

Pride is the key to evil because pride is essentially competitive. Lusts are bad enough, but the things we desire have mostly to do with our bodies. Thus lust does not partake of the essence of evil. Jesus had no difficulty hobnobbing with thieves and prostitutes. His problem lay with the Pharisees and theologians—the proud religious leaders of his day. And the reason for this is that pride is a spiritual evil, infinitely tougher to deal with than bodily evil, infinitely more dangerous. According to the Bible, in fact, it was by pride that evil came into existence. It was, as we have already seen, through an appeal to our pride that humankind fell. We wanted to be like God. We wanted knowledge—the kind of moral knowledge that comes by experience. Unfortunately, all we gained by obtaining that kind of knowledge was a good look at our own nakedness. It was a discovery that our pride could not tolerate. So we hid. We have been hiding ever since, from God, from our fellows, and from ourselves—hiding from reality, in desperate need of repentance.

Pride is evil because it puts us in competition with our neighbors, even with members of our family and those we love most. Lewis points out, "Each person's pride is in competition with everyone else's pride. It is because I wanted to be the big noise at the party that I am so annoyed at someone else being the big noise.... We say that people are proud of being rich, or clever, or good looking, but they are not. They are proud of being richer, or cleverer, or better looking, than others."[15]

I look back with shame on a certain aspect of my childhood. My parents adopted a lovely little girl when I was a preschooler. I thought I loved the little sister I had thus acquired. Indeed, I *did* love her, but I also resented her. She claimed part of the attention I felt belonged to me.

So I entered into competition with her. As we grew older together, I was determined to outdo and outclass my sister in everything either of us attempted. I even took up knitting at one point, knitting myself a sweater of a complicated design, to prove I was better that she—even at feminine things.

I wasn't better, of course, only more skilled in evil. "It cannot be denied," said Victor Hugo in one of his novels, "that one of virtue's phases ends in pride. Therein is a bridge built by the Evil One."[16] I did not realize what I was doing at the time, but in retrospect it is all too cruelly clear. I am ashamed, because in doing what I did, I seriously hurt someone I love.

"Our vices," Lewis adds, "sometimes bring people together: you may find good fellowship and jokes and friendliness among drunken people or unchaste people. But pride always means enmity—it *is* enmity."[17]

The heart of the matter, however, is that pride puts us into competition with God himself. Pride is only comfortable when it can look down on others. And one cannot look down on God. Anyone who truly enters God's presence knows his or her absolute smallness, absolute dependency.

But this raises a problem. I have spoken about the pride of religious people. How is it that they can profess to know God, even to love and serve him, and yet continue in their pride? I can only suppose that in some degree the god they love must be unreal, an imaginary god of their own creating. Anyone can worship a god he or she "is comfortable with." Such gods are really idols. The terrible truth is that it is so easy to deceive oneself about something so central to truth and to living in reality. No wonder we need repentance.

CONQUERING EVIL

We will never conquer evil—at least, not by ourselves. History shows that the Beast in the Basement, the big lie, is too much a part of us, too ingrained in the fabric of the world for us to overcome. Much of the time, by means of law and social structures, we manage to keep its most violent aspects under control. But even then, the lusts and pride that spawned the beast remain at large, living even among the best of us. (Thus Christians make quips about "being so proud of" their humility.)

We cannot conquer evil, especially in ourselves. Most of the time, we cannot even see through the lie, because the lie has permeated our lives.

We cannot *make* ourselves repent, therefore. The impetus for change has to come from outside ourselves. We will explore how this happens in a later chapter. First, however, I want to examine the human mechanisms designed to point us toward repentance: guilt, fear, and conscience.

FIVE

Swimming with God's Tide: How Repentance Works

"I thought," she said, "that I was carried in the will of Him I love, but now I see I walk with it." **C.S. Lewis**

REPENTANCE MAKES CHANGE WORK. As we have seen, no real and lasting change of life direction is possible without the about-face caused by this inner earthquake. But how does repentance work? What happens to us when the ground of our being is shaken enough to make us really change?

Part of the answer can be found in the climax of the classic change-story I began in chapter three, the story of the prodigal son. As you recall, I said the title is a poor one, because it is really the father's story more than the son's. So what about the father? What did he do when his wayward son "came to himself" and journeyed home?

Jesus said, "But while he was still a long way off, his father saw him and was filled with compassion for him; he ran to his son, threw his arms around him and kissed him (Lk 15:20)."

How was it the father spotted the son far off in the dis-

tance? Probably he spotted him *because he was looking for him.*
For years, from the flat roof of the farmhouse, he has
scanned the horizon. His hopes have risen many times, only
to be dashed to the ground. Then at last his old heart begins
to quicken again. Is that his boy? It could be... no... but wait
a minute—yes, it *is!*

The old man begins to run. He stumbles down to the main
floor, shouting orders to the servants who come trailing after
him. But his eyes are only on the son. There is no pause as
they come together. The boy begins the little speech he has
prepared: "Father, I have sinned against heaven and against
you. I am no longer worthy to be called your son (Lk
15:21)."He gets no further. The father's arms are around him,
and he is shouting to the servants, "Quick! Bring the best
robe and put it on him! Put a ring on his finger and sandals
on his feet! Bring the fatted calf and kill it. Let's have a feast
and celebrate. For this son of mine was dead and is alive
again; he was lost and is found (Lk 15:22-24)."

REPENTANCE: THE JOURNEY BACK TO GOD

There is more to the story. Why, then, do I always weep
when I get this far? Probably for a complexity of reasons. For
one thing I understand from painful personal experience
how the father feels. In addition, I myself have a deep longing for a father's love, and I am inclined never to be sure
whether I'll get it or not. I know I never deserve it.

Yet Jesus is in fact telling the story to show us how God re-
acts to our repentance. For whether we know it or not, the father in this story represents God the Father of us all, with
whom we really are dealing when we repent. Coming to
ourselves, aligning ourselves with the moral structure of the
universe, facing up to reality is always, in essence, going *back*
to God—whether we call it that or not—for his were the

hands that shaped us in our mothers' wombs. Returning to him, for the first time or the fiftieth, can be hard, but there is no other way to a profound and positive change of character.

Going back to God. This is how C. S. Lewis defines repentance: "It is simply a description of what going back to Him is like. If you ask God to take you back without it, you are really asking him to let you go back without going back. It cannot happen."[1]

And when we do start home, we are inevitably greeted with love—the kind of love that unceasingly stares at the horizon from the roof top, the kind of love that runs with frantic abandon to embrace us, the kind of love that perseveres in the face of our stupidity.

Not that it's easy. The hardest thing any of us will ever have to do in life is start on that homeward journey. Our stubbornness and pride rise up. The habit of proud independence is hard to break. The way of transgressors is hard, yet no one wants to admit they have chosen the wrong route. Rather than admit we are wrong—or that there is something wrong with us—we would prefer to suffer, to get lost, to waste our time and our lives. Yet once we have said it, admitted that we have been traveling in the wrong direction, then, and not until then, there comes an easing.

In chapter one, you may remember, I mentioned that the Bible uses more than one word to describe repentance. The New Testament word *metanoia* has to do with the changed way of looking at things. But the Old Testament word *nocham* carries a connotation of an easing, an entering into comfort. That seems strange to some people. How can it be comforting to look our own shortcomings, even our own evil, in the face?

Repentance is comforting because of what happens afterward. The prodigal son had only to admit what he had done, what he had become, and then he was able to start home. In a sense, the comfort of repentance is the kind of comfort you get when you stop banging your head against a wall! But it is also the comfort of coming home to the open arms of your Father.

REPENTANCE: REJOINING THE HUMAN RACE

This brings us to a second important point about how repentance happens: it always takes place *in relation to someone*—perhaps to God alone, more likely to someone else as well. Repentance is never just a private affair, but an interpersonal one. It will always involve a turning in vulnerability and in weakness to someone we have wronged, and ideally to God himself as we do so. No profound change can take place without this.

"I am a rock. I am an island!" Simon and Garfunkle charmed us with the song which was a take-off from John Donne's famous dictum: "...every man is a piece of the continent, a part of the main." Simon and Garfunkle were products of a world that still bases its views on individualism. We say, "That's his (or her) problem!" implying that the problem has nothing to do with us. We stand on our own feet.

But we are mistaken. Donne is right.

When I feel miserable and want to be alone, I affect the whole family. A cloud of gloom descends on everyone. They may say, "That's *his* problem," but that is only their way of defying a basic fact of life—that we are part of one another. We influence one another, depend on one another.

We were never more a part of one another than in the technological society of which we are a part—and never more foolish than to deny the fact. Yet it is a fact of life deeper than technology, recognized by every primitive society. Consequently we have duties to one another, and even by our neglect and indifference, can injure one another.

We say, for example, that alcoholics hurt only themselves. To be sure, their behavior is self-destructive. Nevertheless,

every alcoholic leaves a trail of damaged relationships behind—a boiling wake of angry and resentful people.
Spouses, friends, parents, children, helpers all suffer wrong.
They may cut themselves free from any association with the
apparently incorrigible wretch who has hurt them, but their
lives have been profoundly affected. Behind even the story
of the solitary drunk, a hurting someone lurks in the shadows. AA knows this. Their philosophy calls for the alcoholic
to face and put right all those wrongs that can be righted, as
part of the straightening out process.[2]

Whether we like it or not, we are part of the web of life,
part of its weaving. The death of anyone robs and impover-
ishes us. The birth of a baby always enriches us. Our every
word and action affects someone. Therefore when we repent,
it must be in relation to someone. It is not enough just to admit our failings privately. We must become honest with
other people and with God before lasting change can begin.

The vulnerability of repentance is what frightens us the
most. I believe there is a sense in which we cannot ever rectify any wrong we have ever done. Even if we return property we have stolen, apologize for slander, or try to make up
for neglect—the wounds we have inflicted on others may
never be healed in this life. Nevertheless, we must turn toward whomever we have wronged to acknowledge the mess
we have created, the harm or hurt for which we are responsible.

Christians especially need to realize this interdependence.
Reared in a culture where individualism is cherished, we fail
to realize how unhuman individualism is, how destructive
to our humanity and our relationships with others. Facing
our weaknesses, facing the wrongs we have done others, entering into a relationship with Someone greater than ourselves—all these are necessary for true change.

Oswald Chambers writes: "You only reach your real identity when you are merged with another person. When love,
or the Spirit of God strikes a man, he is transformed, he no

longer insists on his separate individuality. Our Lord never spoke in terms of individuality, of... isolated position, but in terms of personality—'that they may be one, even as We are one.'"[3]

Let me repeat, there is no such thing as private sin or private evil. I may fool myself into believing, for instance, that my "private" feelings of hatred toward my parents hurt nobody but me. But "private" feelings change me. They change me in all my relationships, in some degree robbing everyone I meet of aspects of my person to which they are entitled.

Yes, *entitled*. None of us has a right to live to himself or herself. We live and die before and to our fellow human beings and God. Repentance is a doorway to a true joining, not only with God, but with the human race. Only in this way can it be an agent of profound and positive change in us.

REPENTANCE: WILLPOWER OR GRACE?

None of these fundamental facts about repentance, however, speaks to the basic question of where change comes from. Anyone who has ever tried to make a major lifestyle change or even break a simple habit knows that just making up one's mind to change usually is not enough.

In chapter two, I indicated that repentance results from a build-up of inner tensions, and that repentance is the inner earthquake that releases those tensions. But where does the impulse for the earthquake originate? And what determines if the build-up of tensions will result in positive change, rather than mental or emotional collapse?

Remember Chuck Colson, weeping in his parked car? The productive changes that followed his own inner earthquake were ample proof that he was not falling apart mentally. No, something had happened to him that was more than a stress crisis. Chuck Colson had seen something. It was as yet unclear to him, however dazzling in its power—and very clearly from outside of himself. Somehow, he realized he must humble himself and submit to that something—that Someone.

Repentance is a gift of God's grace—and he pours out that grace on all men and women. The sun shines on every farmer's fields. Everyone's crops are watered when rain falls. And when drought comes, it comes as part of the merciful judgments of God. Terrible as they may seem, God's desire is to draw us back to himself. He is the Father, searching the horizon for our return. He speaks in kindness, but sometimes he needs to "shout" by letting us reap the painful consequence of our stupidity. God the Father pours love and truth on all, whether we know and acknowledge it or not. He is the force that triggers the release of repentance.

However, truth is something we have to be willing to receive. Repentance, remember, almost always involves painful insights about ourselves. When the "earthquake" hits, our understanding grows larger; we grasp something new—and we usually don't like it. Charles Finney writes, "To one who truly repents, sin looks like a different thing from what it does to him who has not repented."[4]

Inevitably, then, the role of a person's will—or *volition*—is critical in repentance, even if the impulse of repentance is God-given. You have to be willing to see the new reality being opened up to you, so your changed view is partly a matter of your own decision. However, you may not *feel* you made any decision. Sometimes, it seems almost as though the decision made itself and you became aware of it after it had happened.

At other times you make a clear and conscious decision, but in the teeth of despair. Then a considerable length of time may elapse before the changes begin. The decision may thus be a grim grappling with sails and rudder in the teeth of a gale before you can limp into harbor. There is no fixed pattern.

How, then, does the human will figure in repentance?

"Willpower" is often cited as a key to change—and often decried as the one quality many of us lack. Can we will ourselves to change?

REPENTANCE AND THE HUMAN WILL

When I talk about *will*, I am talking about the human capacity to make decisions. Immediately I face a problem. What part of us is it that makes decisions?

I hinted a moment ago that Chuck Colson, in the moment of his personal earthquake, might not have been able to clearly articulate what was happening to him. I could be wrong, of course. However, it is true that we often make decisions, but realize only in retrospect what was going on in our minds at the time we did so. We may act without knowing why—or without even knowing why we don't know! Sometimes we "rationalize." We invent a reason, fooling ourselves into believing it is the real one.

Thus decisions can be made unconsciously as well as consciously. This is why we sometimes find ourselves doing things we didn't want to do and feeling pulled both ways even as we do something. We also avoid doing things we vowed to ourselves we would do. At a superficial level we say yes, when at a deep level we are saying no—or vice versa. Thus, tension develops between two levels of our being, perhaps building toward the earthquake of repentance.

But repentance and real change also involve a decision. How is that decision made? Who makes it? A theologian once said to me, "Repentance is exclusively a human matter. It is something *I* do, not something God does." Was he right?

It doesn't *look* that way. It wasn't like that with Chuck. It wasn't like that with the Welsh people, who came to grumble to their minister, but who were swept by a common urge to weep. Yet a decision was nevertheless involved at some level. *Overwhelmed* is the word I would use to describe their experience.

But I would not say that their power of choice was overwhelmed (though some psychologists and theologians would argue that it was). Instead, I believe that—seeing the real issues for the first time—they knew, without even having to think about the matter, which side they were on. In this case we are dealing with an unconscious yes overwhelming a conscious no.

LIVING IN THE MIDDLE VOICE

In 1988 Eugene Peterson wrote an article entitled "Growth: An Act of the Will?"[5] In it, he uses three images to explain the kind of question we are facing concerning repentance and the will. They are images drawn from meat cutting, wood carving, and Greek grammar.

Cutting meat is not a purely active process, at least if the meat cutter knows his or her job. A good butcher does not merely use his will to cut up the meat that lies passive and helpless before him. Instead, a butcher *works with* the material he is given—thus submitting to the meat to a certain extent.

The same principle holds true for a good wood carver. What appears outwardly to be an activity arising purely from the carver's decisions is in fact a form of collaboration between the carver and a particular block of wood. Varying densities in the block, the direction of the grain, the position of knotholes, and other irregularities influence him as to the shape of the final carving.

This principle works in many other pursuits as well. A sailor works together with the wind and the waves, a skier with slopes and snow, and so forth.

For me, however, Peterson's most illuminating illustration

is his account of his struggle to understand "the middle voice" in Greek. Eventually light dawned and he described his new understanding as follows: "When I speak in the middle voice, I actively participate in the results of an action that another initiates: 'I take counsel.'"[6]

What exactly is Peterson saying? Don't be put off by terms like "middle voice" or thoughts of classical Greek. Think again of wood carving and meat cutting.

Repentance, remember, is an interpersonal affair, and one that essentially always has to do with God. Repentance is something like "taking counsel"—actively reaching out for something God initiates. In the quotation, Peterson speaks of counsel and counseling. Picture yourself at the receiving end in the office of a counselor. You talk at length, while the counselor murmurs the sort of thing that counselors tend to murmur—encouraging background noises.

Finally the counselor says, "Um, ah—it seems to me that what you are saying is.... But wouldn't you also agree that...?" Now the counselor is actively giving counsel.

At this point you can adopt one of three attitudes. You can let the counselor push you around, that is, dictate your course for you. In this case, you will be taking a passive approach—what could be called *the passive voice*.

Or you can refuse to accept what the counselor is saying. You can mentally call him or her an idiot (your assessment could be right or wrong), and determine to go your own way. Rather than be passive in the face of the counselor's advice, you could take *the active voice*, refusing the counsel.

Peterson's explanation represents a third alternative: "You could *take* counsel." In *the middle voice*, you neither passively get pushed along by the counselor's advice nor actively resist it. Instead, you listen to it. Puzzle over it, perhaps. Then something happens. A light comes on, an "Oh, I see what you are saying now! Gosh—you may well be right, you know. I never saw that!" And you choose to embrace the advice as something you have now seen for yourself. You realize at once which course *the real part of you* wants to follow. That is, you realize what you want at the most fundamental level of your being.

Peterson tells us that our lives were meant to be lived "in the middle voice." By that he means that we see and embrace what God is showing us. We are neither the masters of our fate nor the passive victims of it.

External forces impinge on our lives, and the greatest of these is the Force that molded us in the wombs of our mothers. It—or rather he—is not a vague and abstract "higher power," but a personal and loving Creator—one who could readily override our wills if he so chooses, even if he rarely does.

In the face of *that* Force, impinging on us day and night, hour after hour, and yet leaving us free to choose our own way—we must live in the middle voice. We must actively participate in the results of his actions. To do so is to live in continual repentance.

The God I believe in is the God of the earthquake, of the tornado, and yet of the gentlest breeze. He may sometimes use volcanic violence from within us to get our attention, but he prefers that we collaborate with his subtlest promptings. In our fear and mistrust we pull against him, like untrained oxen, unaccustomed to his yoke.

Living in the middle voice is the result of discovering we can trust God.

CHILDISH DEFIANCE AND CHILDLIKE TRUST

Living in "the middle voice" involves the active use of our wills. But willpower can be used in a way that is the antithesis of what I am advocating. Such an attitude is described in William Ernest Henley's famous poem, "Invictus." The stubborn stoicism of these verses has the power to send shivers of excitement through me. And yet they reflect an attitude which is just the opposite of the one we need if we are to change for the better:

> Out of the night that covers me,
>   Black as the pit from pole to pole,
> I thank whatever gods may be
>   For my unconquerable soul.
>
> In the fell chance of circumstance
>   I have not winced nor cried aloud,
> Under the bludgeonings of chance
>   My head is bloody, but unbow'd.
>
> It matters not how strait the gate,
>   How charged with punishments the scroll,
> I am the master of my fate:
>   I am the captain of my soul.[7]

This poem reflects more than life in "the active voice." It reflects an attitude of defiance toward the forces that challenge the author. The reason it sends shivers down my spine is that there is a part of me that would dearly love to play the defiant and bloodied hero.

Yet the stance the poet assumes is absurd. It is the dramatic posturing of a troubled child rebelling against an adult world. The poet's defiance appeals to the troubled child in me. But it just doesn't stand in the face of reality. Maturity as an adult brings with it an acceptance of my smallness before the vast forces of the universe. At its best, it includes a childlike trust in the universe's Creator.

We do *not* live our lives in a vacuum—or on a stage by ourselves. We are surrounded not only by other people, but by invisible forces both malign and beneficent, by natural energies, and by the powers of heaven and of hell. All of these constantly affect us, whether we know it or not. And we cannot change for the better until we learn to work with that fact.

Most important of all, we must recognize—consciously or unconsciously, that we "live, move, have our being" *in God himself* (Acts 17:28). To quote Peterson again: "I enter into the action which was begun by another, my creating and saving Lord, and find myself participating in the results of the action. I neither do it nor have it done to me; I will to participate in what is willed."[8]

PLUNGING INTO LIFE'S OCEAN SWELLS

C.S. Lewis expresses this concept of participation in a novel that has been variously entitled *Perelandra* and *Voyage to Venus*. The hero, Ransom, arrives on the planet Venus to discover that its surface is largely ocean—an ocean dotted with floating islands. The waves are huge (hundreds of feet high), but the islands ride smoothly up and down the waves.

On one of the islands, Ransom meets "the lady"—a sort of Eve, who is a strange blend of innocence and curiosity. A mishap has separated her from her husband, "the king," the only other inhabitant of the planet. She is at first disappointed when she meets Ransom, having hoped when she saw him in the distance that her husband had returned.

But the lady quickly recovers from her disappointment, believing that God (called *Maleldil* on Venus), who sends only good, must have some good purpose in her meeting with Ransom. Far more important than the love of her husband is the guiding principle of her life: her absolute trust in the wisdom and goodness of Maleldil.

Her disappointment at seeing only Ransom, and her recovery from it, lead her to the insight expressed in the quotation that heads this chapter: "'I thought,' she said, 'that I was carried in the will of Him I love, but now I see I walk with it.

I thought that the good things He sent me drew me into them as the waves lift the islands; but now I see that it is I who plunge into them with my own legs and arms, as when we go swimming.'"[9]

God will have it no other way. Passivity will get us nowhere. He calls us to dynamic interaction, to plunge into the waves he sends to us—with our own arms and legs, day by day, moment by moment. We are not to sit passively on an island whose waves lift and carry us. We are called to *will to participate in what is willed*, as Peterson would put it.

Now, some people might say, "I think I understand. This would involve exercising my will to put into practice everything that is found in the Bible. But that's exactly where my problem lies. I've tried it—and I can't."

That is not at all what I mean. True, we should put every good thing we know into practice. How different things would be if we did! But I agree: we are unable to do so. We are not the masters of our fate, the captains of our souls. We are swimmers meeting the waves that come to us.

More accurately, in repentance we are children plunging for the first time into the waves. If we are to succeed at swimming, we need more than the will to swim. What we need is a teacher, preferably a dad who can support us and instruct us while we learn to kick.

Repentance involves learning. I need to interpret the movement of the water and how it relates to my strokes and my own buoyancy. As I learn to move through the water and to react appropriately to the movement of the waves, I begin to ride atop them with less effort.

So it is with repentance and the lifestyle changes that follow. I need to sense the forces that I encounter, the good and evil which impinges on my spirit. I need to know how to interpret what is happening to me and to sense and collaborate with the power of God. I need to ski with my senses tuned to snow and changing slope, to sail with every nerve attuned to the changing wind. For this is what is going on when we live in the middle voice.

Let me return to the moment of repentance. I have referred to it as a new way of seeing reality, and I have indicated that such a moment requires a decision—conscious or unconscious. But the question arises: Do I make the decision because I begin to see things differently? Or do I see things differently because I have made the decision?

I am not sure that I know. It would be neater and perhaps more satisfactory to say that the decision to change comes first and that the seeing with new eyes follows. But I am inclined to believe that in reality both are true. I make a decision because I see things differently, but I also begin to see things differently because I have made a decision. The process becomes progressive, ongoing, cyclical: deciding, then seeing with fresh eyes; seeing with fresh eyes, then making decisions.

CHANGE FROM OUTSIDE OURSELVES

In any event, supernatural influences are the original impulse for any deep and lasting change. Chuck Colson's feeling of bodily heat on the veranda of the Phillips' house and subsequent sense in the car that his whole being was being "bathed" tell me that Chuck experienced more than a mere emotional reaction. The "something" that was present in the Welsh chapel, that neither the diarist, nor anyone else "had ever before felt," convinces me of the same in the case of the Welsh Christians. The "something" may not always be experienced or consciously felt, but I am convinced it is always present in true repentance.

The founders of AA (who were Christians) knew this, although they never came right out and said so. When the movement was founded, however, there was even more resistance to anything having to do with God than there is now. Many alcoholics came from homes where the word "God" was associated with hypocrisy on the part of parents, ministers, and others they knew. If *that* was all there was to God-talk, they wanted no more of it.

Therefore the AA founders, knowing the knee-jerk reaction of many alcoholics to religious jargon, opted for "God as you understand him" language. I'm not sure they were right. I would prefer to see other biblical elements added to the Twelve Steps. (I shall attempt to do this in chapters 10-12.)

And yet I have to concede that AA and its sister organizations do far more effective work with alcoholics and other addicts than churches do. As a matter of fact, I know that many alcoholics experience real, deep, and lasting character change that began in AA.

Why is this? I believe it is because God is less squeamish about the agencies he uses in drawing people to himself than some of his followers are. God loves people—so much that he is not above using people and institutions whose theological understanding is limited or defective in order to draw wounded people to himself.

Betty's repentance took place in AA. Through the acute stages of her recovery period, she knew what it was to hear God's voice. Only later did she enter into an understanding of her relationship with Jesus. Before she had any grasp of the God who had lovingly acted in her life, the God to whom she was responding, Betty had already begun to "live life in the middle voice." And her story is typical of many others like her. It does not follow, however, that *all* addicts who work through the Twelve Steps—not even all those who live in recovery—become Christians or develop a relationship with God. As I have indicated, repentance is a God-given human mechanism available to all—and the divine influence that triggers repentance moves in the lives of every person.

In describing this phenomenon, Christian theologians

speak of *prevenient grace*. It is a phrase they use to remind us that the work of the Holy Spirit[10] begins long before people become Christians.

When prevenient grace begins to be imparted, people are rarely aware that it is God with whom they are dealing. When God first begins his work in people's lives, never for a moment do they dream what is really happening as certain thoughts and feelings float through their minds.

In addition, many—perhaps most—people to whom the Holy Spirit ministers never become Christians—or even make other changes they need to make in their lives. All of us have the choice of rejecting or responding to what is happening to us. There are stages in God's dealing with us, successive stages depending on our response. That is why repentance is normally a prelude to change, and why real and lasting change must always include deep repentance.

BUTTERFLIES THAT NEVER FLY: A THEOLOGY OF CONVERSION

This is especially of the specific and important kind of change known as Christian *conversion*, the behavioral reorientation that can follow the acceptance of Christian beliefs. As I pointed out in an earlier chapter, repentance is not the same thing as conversion; repentance precedes conversion. But the pain and release of repentance is necessary for conversion to be deep and complete.

If you watch a butterfly as it struggles its way out of cocoon, you may feel tempted to help it out with a pair of scissors. Sticky strands of goo seem to hold back the butterfly's progress. As its wings begin to unfurl in the sunlight, similar strands impede their full development.

Yet these struggles of metamorphosis are necessary. Without the hindrances and the struggles to overcome them, the wings will never develop properly. Your "help" will only produce a cripple, incapable of flight.

Christians who have never known repentance are like butterflies that have never flown. Many Christians cannot "fly" because the process by which they became Christians was defective. Some were given an intellectual understanding of one or two basic facts about Christ's redemptive work and encouraged on that basis to believe on him. Others were baptized in infancy and later given a similar understanding before they were confirmed.

But commonly absent is any deep heart awareness of the appalling nature of what their lives would be like without him. What the Holy Spirit may have begun in prevenient grace gets short-circuited by the Christian "system."

I am not deploring the various modes of entry into the Christian church. All I am saying is that often those who are responsible for the evangelizing or counseling process have themselves understood little about the purposes and function of true repentance.

For this reason, anxious to "process" others as they themselves have been processed, they do exactly what we might be tempted to do when we see the struggles of a butterfly emerging from a cocoon. They fail to grasp adequately that God is at work in butterflies and in human souls alike. Insensitive to his working, they trust the process or the system we are used to. In so doing we often produce Christians "who cannot fly"—even some who may not have saving faith at all.

Coming to faith by the "scissors" route is dramatically different from turning to God in repentance. Usually there are no tears, no deathly struggle to face the appalling sight of our sin, no mourning. Consequently there is less subsequent joy and triumph, less possibility of profound change in character.

I am not speaking here of emotionalism—deliberately playing on the emotions of "prospects" as the Maoist teachers in the Chinese university did and some evangelists are prone to do. Emotionalism consists of another kind of interference—an artificial attempt to reproduce the picture that people have seen during revivals, merely another way of snipping the sticky goo with a pair of scissors.

Not only Christian preachers and counsellors, but psychologists and psychiatrists as well make the same mistake. Many so-called therapies focus on the surface symptoms while ignoring the underlying pathology. The change in behavior that follows tends to be short lived. Similarly, diet regimens that publish before and after pictures rarely show follow-up pictures. What size of dress does the lady wear two years later? (Usually a size larger than the one she wore before going on the diet.)

Behavioral psychology is quite open about this tendency to focus on surface behavior. "Mind" is regarded as a black box, whose contents are deliberately ignored by orthodox behaviorists. After all, the contents of the mind are hard to measure, and therefore do not come under the bailiwick of science.

Behavioral psychology does produce results. But in many cases the results are not permanent. The black box is much more than a black box. It used to be called a soul.

God's side of the work in a human soul cannot be reproduced by human techniques of any sort. Such human techniques as develop arise from inadequate awareness of or insensitivity to God's part in human change.

Whether the change is Christian conversion or another turning in lifestyle, it begins with the grace of God moving us toward repentance. It is up to us to cooperate with that grace or to ignore it. And that decision—whether conscious or unconscious—is something no one else can make for us.

Changes in our lives do involve other people. But the underlying decision that shakes the bedrock of my life is always a matter for myself and God.

THE PULL OF GRACE

I talked earlier about the prevenient grace of God. Whether you recognize it or not, God is already on to your case. You will know that fact by any sense of dissatisfaction or desire for change. Desire for improvement, however feeble, does not originate in yourself. It is the beckoning of a divine finger, a pull of divine love and longing.

God's beckoning finger can take an infinite variety of forms. It can be painful or joyful, a weariness that cries for rest, an anticipation that awakens hope, a tension that cries out for peace, a sense of guilt that haunts.

Guilt is particularly common. Because of the complexities of its mechanisms, we will look at it in the next chapter.

SIX

The Psychology of Conscience

Thus conscience does make cowards of us all...
William Shakespeare

[Robert Louis Stevenson] could treat his conscience as cavalierly as most men: but, like all of us, he could neither implicitly obey it, nor effectively silence it.
John Kellman, from the introduction to
The Strange Case of Dr. Jekyll and Mr. Hyde

Guilt and conscience are two words often associated with repentance. Some would even say they cause repentance—that we are moved to change because we feel guilty or because our conscience bothers us. But while that interpretation includes a grain of truth, it is fundamentally inaccurate.

Guilt feelings and conscience are indeed closely related to repentance, but they do not bring it about. Indeed, repentance may be necessary in order for our sense of guilt and our conscience to function as they should. For both these two barometers of right and wrong are part of our human makeup. As such, they are subject to the same distortions as any human faculties. Even our sense of right and wrong is often in need of deep-seated change!

101

THE TORMENTING VOICE OF CONSCIENCE

Conscience is closely related to what psychoanalysts refer to as superego. The two terms are not identical because they arise from different purposes. Psychoanalysts are concerned with how superego arises, what can go wrong with it, and how the wrong can be righted, rather than on the moral reality affecting it.[1]

Nevertheless, the terms *conscience* and *superego* cover the same category of experience: the mental and emotional messages that tell us whether our actions are right or wrong.

As most of us know from personal experience, an aroused conscience can torment us and make us miserable. The great French novelist Victor Hugo, in his masterpiece *Les Miserables,* vividly describes such agony in the life of his central character, Jean Valjean. He learns one day that another man faces death for crimes which he himself has committed. The accused is similar in appearance to Valjean and has been wrongly identified by witnesses.

Valjean is living under an assumed name. Lacking any trust in the nineteenth-century French justice system, Valjean is convinced that the accused man will certainly die if he does not come forward and identify himself. Hugo describes the criminal's inner conflict:

By some strange impulse of almost inexplicable anxiety, he rose from his chair and bolted his door. He feared lest something might yet enter. He barricaded himself against all possibilities.

A moment afterward he blew out his light. It annoyed him. It seemed to him that somebody could see him.

Who? Somebody?

Alas! What he wanted to keep outdoors had entered; what he wanted to render blind was looking upon him. His conscience.

His conscience, that is to say, God.[2]

We may never have behaved in the same way Valjean did. Nevertheless we can understand his actions. We know the haunting struggle to hide from the accusing finger of our own consciences. Shakespeare is right that conscience turns us into cowards. "My conscience has thousand several tongues," Richard III cries, "And every tongue brings in a several tale. And every tale condemns me for a villain."[3]

Shakespeare and Hugo are both correct when they declare that our consciences can create torment in us. But Hugo is wrong when he identifies God with our conscience. God's view of right and wrong is the standard; it reflects his unchangeable character. In contrast, we were born with unreliable consciences, and our upbringing has not made them any more accurate. If God were our conscience, we would all agree about right and wrong. Obviously this is not the case. One person feels free to do what someone else would never dream of doing. But if conscience is not the voice of God inside us, then what is conscience?

When we feel guilty we may say, "I've got a guilty conscience," or, "My conscience is bothering me." Conscience, then, is the name we give to something in us that approves of us when we do right and makes us feel anxious and guilty when we do what we think is wrong. It is an element of our consciousness that functions as a kind of barometer of right and wrong. But as we will see, the conscience—or superego—can be an unreliable guide.

THE CHANGEABLE CONSCIENCE

John Bunyan, author of the classical allegory, *The Pilgrim's Progress,* wrote a second book in which he vividly depicted the changeable nature of conscience. *The Holy War* tells the story of the city of Mansoul, a city built by the great King Shaddai. The evil Prince Diabolus enters Mansoul by guile and treachery and persuades the inhabitants to accept his rule. Eventually King Shaddai's forces led by Captain Boanerges retake the city.

Most of the story concerns the leading citizens of the city and their reactions to the war between the forces of good and evil. One leading citizen is the town Recorder, an old gentleman named Mr. Conscience. Prince Diabolus hates Mr. Conscience, a man "well read in the laws of his king, and also a man of courage and faithfulness to speak the truth.... [He] had a tongue as bravely hung as he had a head filled with [good] judgement." In past times, Mr. Conscience had been the spokesman for King Shaddai, acting as the voice of the ruler to the city. Even under the rule of the usurper, Prince Diabolus, "his words did shake the whole town; they were like the rattling thunder... like thunder-claps."[4]

Fearing Mr. Conscience's influence on the citizens of Mansoul, Prince Diabolus determines to destroy him. He lures the old gentleman with alcohol and gets him frequently drunk. In this way he achieves the twin goals of making Mr. Conscience's judgment unreliable and undermining the confidence of the citizens of Mansoul in his pronouncements. Before long, Mr. Conscience screams warnings of imminent catastrophe at midnight when no danger is near. When danger truly threatens, the Recorder is asleep in a drunken stupor. Gradually the citizens pay him less heed. Bunyan is giving us a picture of the unreliability of our consciences. They can only function when they work properly. Like a watch, a conscience needs to be set accurately (as well as rightly adjusted and cleaned if necessary) so that it "keeps proper time."

But resetting a conscience is infinitely trickier than resetting a watch. I learned that myself early in my adult life. I had been brought up to believe movies were wrong—evil, of the devil. As I matured, however, I reasoned that this was not true. Eventually, I decided to actually go to a movie—as I recall, a black and white film of *The Hound of the Baskervilles*.

But there was a problem. My rational decision that movies

were OK had not really "reset" my conscience properly. I could not sleep that night, tortured with misgivings about my "sin."

Why is resetting a conscience so hard? There are several problems involved. Before we examine them, however, let us look at some of the ways our consciences may become inaccurate.

HYPERSENSITIVE CONSCIENCE

I once had a guilt-haunted friend named Jim who plunged into depression whenever he made a major purchase. He had what psychoanalysts would call a *punitive* superego. A purchase of a house once had him endlessly going to his priest for confession.

His sin? Jim thought he was guilty of cupidity. He had fallen into the sin of wanting to own a house instead of being willing to go on renting. Jim had a good steady job, and his wife also worked. They could easily meet the mortgage payments. Yet he was terrified of the mortgage. "What will happen if I should lose my job?" he asked me with fear-filled eyes. (His job was in no danger; he still works for the same company.)

Jim's anxiety was largely made up of guilt. He felt he had done wrong—that he had disobeyed God. Jim's very religious parents had been brought up during the Depression and had also had a great fear of having no money. They had brought him up to be strict with himself about saving. As a result, though he was a Roman Catholic, he was a model of the so-called Protestant ethic. Jim had been taught that saving pleased God and that debt was sin. "Owe no man anything… " was a Scripture his parents quoted often (Rom 13:8).

At four years of age, Jim had raided his piggy bank to buy candy. His parents—perhaps fearing that Jim would turn out to be a ne'er-do-well—were furious. Such tendencies would have to be nipped in the bud. They never allowed Jim to forget the incident. The rejection this involved, plus his parents' own obvious fear over money matters, became incorporated into the way Jim's conscience worked. His early experiences had saddled him with a punitive superego. It took Jim three years to get used to the house payments.

Then Jim traded in his old car, which he had driven so long it was practically worthless. At first the business of purchasing a new one went very well. The light of joy shone in Jim's eyes when he drove his wife home in the brand new (but modest) compact he so badly needed. Yet that same night we received a telephone call. "John, I knew deep down I was doing wrong in buying this car. It was pride, just sheer pride that made me buy it. D'you think they'd take it back? I feel awful!"

Jim's conscience had been shaped less by godly principles than by early experiences of parental fears and rejection. It had been artificially inflamed, just as the consciences of the Chinese students (mentioned in chapter one) had been at the mass rallies organized by the communists. As a result, his conscience was hypersensitive, reading "guilty" even in instances where Jim was not at fault.

SEARED WITH HOT IRONS

Conscience—as in Jim's case—can be too sensitive. But it can also be not sensitive enough. After all, it is meant to function. Its purpose is neither to condemn nor exonerate, but to serve as a guide to life's deepest realities and to motivate healthy behavior. In particular, it is meant to be a source of certainty in knowing. The Greek word used for it in the New Testament is *suneidesis*—to know with oneself.

The apostle Paul writes about *weak* consciences, the consciences of people like Jim who feel guilty when there is no need to do so. But Paul also writes about some people whose consciences have been "seared with a hot iron" (1 Tm 4:2).

For a period in my life I worked with leprosy patients. One of the effects of Hansen's disease (the technical term for leprosy) is to destroy the nerve endings. Leprosy patients therefore often have insensitive skin, and this makes them especially vulnerable. They may place their hands in boiling water and get burned because they felt no pain. They may cut or scrape the exposed parts of their bodies as they work and fail to treat the injuries. Wearing only sandals, or going barefoot, their feet may be cut, grazed, or blistered.

Whereas you or I would react immediately to the pain and take appropriate measures, it may be some time before the leprosy patient even realizes what has happened. In the meantime, burns and other injuries can become infected and ulcerate. On hands and feet, the resulting sores can lead eventually to the loss of fingers and toes, as infection invades other tissues and even bone.

The skin's nerve endings are there for a purpose. They are protective; they enable us to care for and preserve our bodies. Severe burns are similar to leprosy, in that they can destroy the sensitive nerve endings in skin.

Thus a conscience "seared with a hot iron" is an insensitive conscience. The persistent pursuit of evil will progressively deaden the "nerve endings" of the conscience. Evil is moral leprosy, destroying moral sensitivity so that moral pain is lessened. And while this may relieve discomfort, it can lead to a progressive deterioration in our person. Just as patients with Hansen's disease lose parts of their bodies, so we begin to lose essential features of our true personhood, particularly our capacity to know God.

I proved this principle in a minor degree with the movies. I didn't let my wakeful night of conscience-battling curtail my cinema visits. The more I went, the more easily I could sleep afterwards.

Remember Dr. Jekyll and Mr. Hyde? Jekyll's increasing facility in getting into his Hyde form and his increasing difficulty in returning symbolizes what I am talking about. Even more clearly, the example of serial murderers such as Ted Bundy show the internal disaster and the societal chaos that can result from a hardened or seared conscience.

But it is at this point that the analogy of seared nerves, or of nerve endings destroyed by disease, breaks down. Guilt can be experienced again. Long-dead consciences can be awakened. If we are talking of nerve endings—in this case they can grow and become sensitive again.

In my early psychiatric reading I came across beautiful descriptions of people called psychopaths, but in the whole of my experience never met anyone who matched the classic description. To be sure, many people had ineffective consciences. In many, the difficulty arose from inappropriate parental discipline from an early stage. Yet always there has been in my experience of so-called psychopaths the capacity not only to fake a sense of guilt, but actually to experience it.

I believe conscience never actually dies. It may go into profound slumber. But it can be awakened. Colson had progressively desensitized his conscience for years, but on that fateful night at Tom Phillips' house, it was powerfully aroused.

THE DIFFICULTIES OF RESETTING A CONSCIENCE

Hypersensitive consciences or seared, insensitive ones—both represent dangerous distortions of truth. At their farthest extremes, these distortions can develop into psychosis. In their lesser manifestations, they can keep us from experiencing God's best. In order for lasting and positive change to take place, these distorted consciences must be "reset." But as I learned in my experience with the movies, it's not that easy.

The problem of resetting a conscience is actually twofold. First, there is the problem of standards. When you set a watch, you have some standard to set it by. National standards are set by international conventions, and these in turn are based on the regular movements of heavenly bodies. Our opinions and feelings do not affect the movements of these bodies. They are external to us and to our world. We simply measure the accuracy of our clocks by them. Radio, telephone, and television reflect these standards, so that it is easy to adjust our clocks and watches.

Setting a conscience is infinitely trickier. Science provides no international standards of right and wrong. Even if science did, the standards would simply reflect the opinions and traditions of fallible human beings.

So what do we do about standards? Over the past fifty years or so, more and more behavioral scientists have adopted a relativistic stance. For scientific purposes, they have adopted the view that right and wrong are a matter for the individual to judge. Psychologists and psychiatrists will not even say what behavior is *normal*. Statistics show what is *usual*, not what is normal in the sense of appropriate and healthy.

(Of course, you have only to stamp hard and deliberately on the toe of a behavioral scientist to call his or her neutral stance into question. We all object to behavior that damages us, whatever philosophical view we hold.)

The late Donald Gray Barnhouse, a former Philadelphia pastor, used another "time" analogy to show the need for standards in "setting" a conscience. "For a sundial to work properly," he used to say, "you need light, and light from the correct source. You can walk round a sun dial at midnight with a flashlight—and it will tell you anything you want."

According to this analogy, then, my conscience needs light as well as standards. By itself, conscience is likely to supply us with inaccurate—or, at best, unreliable—moral information. Scripture, illuminated by God's Spirit, represents light from the proper source to illuminate conscience.

But there is a second problem—the problem I hit when I first sneaked into a movie theater. Even with an accurate standard, it is far more difficult to "reset" a conscience than a watch, because the origins of our conscience may be buried deep in our early experience. As my experience with the movies shows, we cannot realign our consciences simply by making intellectual decisions as to what is right or wrong— even if those decisions are based on an accurate standard.

Our consciences were shaped partly by the way we were brought up. Animals and small children do not experience conscience so much as fear of reprisal—the awareness that their actions will arouse anger and perhaps even rejection if they are caught. They may therefore feel uneasy or anxious when they do something their elders disapprove.

But the development of conscience is more than the development of an awareness of social approval or disapproval. It is an awareness of cosmic approval or disapproval. The *capacity* for such awareness is innate. But the actual connection of certain actions with this approval or disapproval is learned, and it is not always learned accurately. Thus our early training often impairs our accuracy in knowing right and wrong. It is not only true that we can damage our consciences by defying them, but that they can be wrongly "set" during our childhood. More puzzling still—some children seem to inherit the kind of consciences their parents had.

If as children we learned that regular punishment followed certain actions, then those actions will probably produce guilty feelings in us. If our parents showed rage or even rejection in handling our behavior, then our consciences may be hypersensitive to our faults. Guilt and shame will haunt our days, even waking us in the darkness.

Behind every person with a defective conscience stands the specters of controlling, rejecting parents. More unfortunate still, our view of God is inevitably colored by the way our parents treated us. Faulty training may seriously impede our ability to know God's love.

HOW REPENTANCE RESETS CONSCIENCES

There are several ways of handling such deep-set conscience problems, but nothing has a more dramatic effect than the earthquake of true repentance. Contrary to some accusations, healthy repentance does not produce a pathological conscience. As I have shown, it awakens us to reality—moral and otherwise. Repentance begins the realignment of conscience.

Repentance also deals with the unconscious fears that plague consciences damaged by parental severity or irresponsibility. For as we have seen, normal behavior can be distorted where fear is involved. We may repress intolerable fears of punishment and rejection, as well as memories associated with it.

Repression is not the same as *suppression*. When you suppress something, you decide not to think about. However, if you are so scared of something that you don't know how to handle it, an unconscious mechanism may take over. The matter disappears from your conscious life. But you have not gotten rid of it. It is still there, under the surface, influencing your behavior in ways you would never guess. But when repentance takes place, there is often an awakening of the circumstances surrounding those buried fears.

But it is what happens next that really makes a difference in resetting conscience. For with that resurfacing of buried fears comes a deep assurance of being loved and accepted, or a very deep awareness (as in Chuck Colson's case) that I *cry out for* the acceptance of a supreme Being. In this way the "watch" may be reset, that is, the conscience can perceive reality more accurately and be less troubled by pathological and often unconscious fears of rejection.

The answer to a guilty conscience, therefore, is not the deadening that comes from repeatedly going against that conscience—but the forgiveness, cleansing, and the knowledge that I am loved and accepted again. In this way conscience can be restored to function properly. Healthy repentance involves not only the pain of knowing who I really am, but the wonder of knowing I am loved and accepted.

HOW CONSCIENCE CAN BRING US TO REPENTANCE

I have said that guilt feelings and conscience do not make repentance happen—and that repentance is often necessary to help "reset" defective consciences.

But there is a sense in which conscience and guilt feelings do lead to repentance. As our inner earthquake progresses, an awakened conscience can be part of the new and awakened view of reality we gain as a result. That newly awakened sense of our truly guilty state, in turn, moves us to change.

We can see the dramatic interrelationship of conscience and repentance in a moving story included in some versions of the Gospel of John (see Jn 8:1-11).[5] It is the story of a woman who had been caught in an immoral act, but also a story of the consciences of the religious scholars and leaders who brought her to Jesus.

Jesus is sitting in the temple courtyard. It is early morning, and a large crowd has gathered to hear his teaching. Suddenly they are interrupted. A group of learned teachers and religious men burst through the crowd, dragging a frightened woman. She has been "taken in adultery—in the very act."

People crane their necks to see what is happening, asking their neighbors what is going on. The self-righteous male leaders quote the law of Moses, which called for putting the woman to death (see Lv 20:10). (Actually, the law called for execution of the man and the woman together, but the doctors of the law fail to point this out.)

But the doctors of the law are not really interested in the woman, much less the man involved (who has presumably been released). Instead, they are interested in putting Jesus on the spot. They are jealous of his popularity with the people, and so they have set what they think is a trap. They ask him what should be done with her.

If Jesus says, "Let her go!" he plays into their hands. In that case he is defying the law of Moses. If, on the other hand he says, "Stone her!"—then he will disappoint the people. They will see him as siding with the religious men who have dragged the woman before him.

But Jesus does not seem to be listening to the religious leaders at all. He is leaning forward, writing in the dust with his finger, a look of absorption on his face. The group holding the woman persist, badgering him with questions. The crowd is fascinated. This is an interesting situation indeed. What will the Master do?

At last he lifts his head and looks at the religious teachers. "If anyone of you is without sin, let him be the first to throw a stone at her," he says, then bends down and goes on writing. One by one, "convicted by their own conscience", the religious leaders slip away, "the older ones first, until only Jesus was left" (KJV). The woman crouches alone before Jesus (KJV v. 7).

Jesus is described as being "left alone." I rather think the "alone" refers to the absence of the men who had been heckling him—that the crowd is still watching. Jesus' calm quietness is no doubt the last thing either the religious leaders or the crowd anticipated. They had been expecting arguments and a verbal and political triumph for one side or other. The crowd has noted each scholar retiring and are doubtless making their own comments.

Jesus lifts his eyes again, "Woman, where are they? Has no one condemned you?"

"No one, sir."

"Then neither do I condemn you. Go now and leave your life of sin."

AWAKENED TO REALITY

What had gone on in the minds of the religious teachers? No one finds it easy to put someone else to death in cold blood. In mob violence you lose your sense that the other person is real. An excitement rises in you, a sort of drunkenness, in which you do things you could never do in ordinary circumstances. But to be faced with someone in the midst of a growing silence, when your own actions are going to be observed by a critical audience, is very different. Perhaps none of the scholars have ever so much as thrown a stone since they were kids.

Jesus has returned the ball to their own court. In effect, he has said, "Go ahead if you want to! Let the holiest one of you pick up the first stone!"

Only someone who has been faced with the situation can really understand what began to happen to the group. It may be that at that point they looked at the woman for the first time. She would still be crouching, perhaps only a couple of feet away. Up to that point she had been merely a stage property, a focus of argument, something to flaunt at Jesus. Now she was a woman, and each of them was a man. Who could pick up the stone that might knock the life out of this woman and leave her a motionless corpse?

The tables were turned. Memories would stir in them. In every age it is remarkable how many religious leaders are involved in sexual sin. As a psychiatrist I used to work with them. How "holy" were these holy men? What memories came back to haunt them? Did each one draw in a breath and think, "*I* cannot batter in her skull. Not after doing what I did that time when... " One by one, struck by their consciences, they had to slip away. But what of the woman?

We are told little about her reactions. In the face of Jesus' calm acceptance, her own conscience must have been flayed raw, her shame and guilt unbearable. I have seen what happens to many people in parallel circumstances. Faced with kindness and acceptance, they repent.

This brings us to an important psychological reality. Although repentance may indeed be painful, it does not come about as a response to severity. Stern accusation and recrimination may exacerbate our feelings of guilt and shame, but they never give rise to true repentance.

Inevitably, it is the wonder of kindness that awakens repentance. Repentance is a concomitant of gratitude and thanksgiving. The relief of knowing we might be loved and accepted is what brings true change. Paul makes this clear as he upbraids his unrepentant readers: "Or do you show contempt for the riches of his kindness, tolerance and patience, not realizing that God's *kindness* leads you toward repentance?" (Rom 2:4).

CONSCIENCE AND GUILT

Conscience—whether accurate or inaccurate—is above all else an arbiter of guilt. It is the mechanism that brings us to an awareness of our guilt.

But what is guilt? At its heart lie two closely related and very powerful emotions. First, there is the fear that the most important people in my life—perhaps the universe itself—will reject me and cast me off. On top of this fear comes a creeping self-loathing, a sense that I am inferior, no good. The fear and the self-hatred are linked. If I am rejected and cast off, I must be loathsome. If I am loathsome, why should I not be cast off?

In the light of such painful feelings, our most basic instinct is to hide. Rather than face the reality of who we are—and thereby be moved to repentance—we tend to fly from reality.

But since we can't really flee from ourselves, we are stuck with the constant bedrock sense of our own inferiority and fear.

Think of the biblical story of the beginnings of humankind recorded in the first few chapters of Genesis. (Even those who have difficulty believing in the literal events have to acknowledge the psychological validity of this picture of how guilt began.)

Until the advent of guilt, we could wander through the world, feeling the grass between our toes and the breeze on every part of our bodies.Even our sexual organs were exposed, and we felt no shame about them. We were infinitely more in touch with the creation of which we are a part than we now are. We were free, joyous, and fearless.

Then came guilt, terror, and shame. "I was afraid because I was naked," Adam mutters as he hides from God among the trees. Only hours before, he had not known what nakedness was, for nakedness is less a state of body than of mind.

Nakedness goes far deeper than our sexuality; it has to do with all that we are. When another person looks upon my naked body with tenderness and no taint of mockery and still accepts me, he or she gives me an incomparable gift. For I was made to know and be known for my naked self. I was made for intimacy—not just bodily intimacy, but intimacy of soul and spirit.

However, when I become alienated and fearful, my impulse is to hide. Clothes create the illusion that my weaknesses and failures are covered, hidden. But in hiding behind cloth and skins, I become alienated from creation, alienated also from my fellows, and alienated from God. My clothes symbolize all that I conceal from you.

Guilt, then, is the beginning of aloneness. And hell, according to C.S. Lewis, is in one sense aloneness taken to the *nth* degree.[6] The torments of hell can be anticipated when we experience pangs of guilt and conscience that make us want to hide and be alone.

I have a need to hide. But I have a greater need—to remove the covering of my soul and to know and be known for who and what I am. Thus I am terrified of the very thing I most want.

At night I may dream of the thing that both fascinates and terrifies me. In my dream I find myself at the city center wearing nothing at all. Dismayed, I seek the covering that perpetually eludes me, wondering how my dilemma came about.

Shame, fear, and guilt make me flee exposure. That elemental fear and self-loathing taught me the terror of nakedness, especially when the floodlights of an awakened conscience expose that nakedness. The terror is greatest when my soul is naked before the dreadful light of God.

We shall never in this life recover the free enjoyment of the relationship between our naked bodies and the rest of creation, although nudist colonies exist for this purpose. To try is to misunderstand the root of the problem—that of evil and unresolved sin.

A certain degree of recovery is possible, however, in repentance. People who have truly repented have no further need to fear others' knowing about the evil that is inside them. In that sense, they can be naked. They do not forget the evil they did, but their experience of pardon is deep enough to end their fear and shame. They can look the rest of us in the eye with joy and confidence.

TRUE GUILT AND FALSE GUILT

One way or another, guilt must be dealt with. If the guilt is false, arising from childhood misperceptions, the conscience must be reset so that awareness of guilt will be more accurate. And as we have seen, this may well require the inner earthquake of repentance.

But it is important to remember that not all guilt is false!

The fact that conscience can be inaccurate does not negate the real presence of evil in the world and in our lives. If our shame and alienation were simply a matter of mistaken ideas instilled in us as children, they would be easy to shake off. They aren't.

In a way, guilt is like a flea, and conscience like the itch arising from flea bites. A fairy story I once wrote for my grandchildren illustrates how guilt must be handled:

The Four Travelers

Once upon a time four travelers sat down in a sandbox that, unbeknown to them, was ridden with fleas. The longer they sat, the more uncomfortable they became, until one by one (each suspecting that the rest would not understand) they rose to their feet and went their separate ways.

The first traveler was walking along the forest glade when he saw an old lady who looked as though she might be a witch of a superior class. "Good Madam," said he, bowing and scratching, "do you have spells to cure itching?"

"I don't sell spells," the old lady returned gravely, "but it is possible that you have a flea. At the end of this path you will find a river lit by the setting sun. Take off your garments and wash them in it. Then jump in yourself and take a bath. When you are clean, cross the river, not by the bridge, but by wading through its deepest part, and put on your clothes on the farther bank."

"Fleas?" thought the first man sensibly as he left the old lady. "Fleas are not very nice to think about. I probably don't have fleas. I'm just imagining things. The best thing I can do is forget about the whole business."

So as he came to the river, he crossed by the bridge with scarcely a downward glance. By and by (he was a strong-minded man) his itching grew less. When last I heard, he was the president of several corporations, housing a whole army of fleas in his underwear but scratching himself only occasionally.

The second traveler followed the highway, but before long he too met the old lady who looked like a witch. "Good Madam," said he, bowing and scratching, "do you have spells to cure itching?"

"I don't sell spells," the old lady returned gravely, "but it is possible that you have a flea. At the end of this path you will find a river lit by the setting sun. Take off your garments and wash them in it. Then jump in yourself and take a bath. When you are clean, cross the river, not by the bridge, but by wading through its deepest part, and put on your clothes on the farther bank."

"Fleas?" said the second traveler as he left the old lady behind. "I don't want to offend the old dear, but who after all is entitled to say what is a flea and what is not? The question is purely relative. In my opinion, fleas exist only in the mind. I admit that I itch, but that's because I was inflicted by punitive parents with a belief in hygienic absolutes."

So saying, he too crossed the bridge over the river whose waters flashed red in the sunset. Later in life, as a psychoanalyst, he amassed a great fortune by taking itches seriously. His flea-bitten patients were told that society had burdened them with a flea complex. The road to freedom was not easy. They must be courageous, defy convention, and sit in a sandbox.

The third traveler saw the old lady, but something about the way she looked at him made him itch all the more. So he went the other way and bought a large bottle of pills at the village drugstore. The pills gave him a lovely, woozy feeling to help him forget the itch. The last I heard of him, he was a famous movie actor, very flea-bitten and woozy most of the time.

The last traveler discovered he had fleas even before the old lady told him. She found him with his shirt off (he blushed when he saw her), dabbing his torso with the moistened tip of his finger, as one of the fleas hopped nimbly out of his way between his shoulder blades. "I'll never get rid of these things," he told her plaintively.

The old lady smiled. "At the end of this path you will find a river lit by the setting sun. Take off your garments and wash them in it. Then jump in yourself and take a bath. When you are clean, cross the river, not by the bridge, but by wading through its deepest part, and put on your clothes on the farther bank."

"Well, there's no harm in trying it," the fourth traveler said. "I'd do anything to get rid of the pests." When he got to the river, he did just as the witch had told him, and rose damp but flealess on the far bank.

Later in life he became a most successful grandfather (far nicer than being a psychoanalyst or a film star) who used to admonish his round-eyed grandchildren with a shake of the finger and the solemn words, "Always get rid of the flea, my dears, and the itch will take care of itself."[7]

That is it. Evil, the source of our true guilt, is a living and inconspicuous thing—like a flea. It came into our world from somewhere else. Evil is also like leprosy: prolonged exposure to it can render us insensitive to the appalling damage that can destroy us.

The whole point of good medical treatment is to treat not just the symptoms, but whatever causes the symptoms. The treatment of the symptoms is well and good, provided one also treats the disease. There is no point in treating itches unless you get rid of the flea.

Conscience gets to be more normal as evil is dealt with. Hypersensitive consciences grow calmer as well as more accurate as they learn the tenderness and compassion God has for us all. Consciences "seared with a hot iron" are awakened again.

In Bunyan's *The Holy War*, it is interesting to note Mr.

Conscience's reactions as the forces of Light begin to invade the city under Captain Boanerges. At first the noise of a battering ram "made the old gentleman shake and totter." And Captain Boanerges' demands for entrance "made the old gentleman tremble the more, yet he durst not but open the gate."[8] Bunyan is describing the awakening of conscience.

As Bunyan's story goes on, the process of recovery in the city Recorder continues. Soon he begins to speak sense again to his fellow citizens: "I, for my part have transgressed greatly, and he that is clean, it is well for him. But I say I have transgressed greatly in keeping silence when I should have spoken, and in perverting justice when I should have executed the same.... Oh! I tremble to think what will be the end of this so dreadful and ireful a beginning![9]

But as we saw in the case of the woman taken in adultery, love and acceptance are the most powerful components in handling a reawakened conscience and bringing about repentance.

THE TRANSFORMING POWER OF ACCEPTANCE

Early in the chapter we observed Jean Valjean's tortured conscience over a man who has been accused of his own crimes. Eventually he goes to the court and confesses, saving the man falsely accused. That he should do so at the prompting of his conscience was inevitable, for earlier in his life he had himself been transformed by profound repentance.

Years before, Valjean had been confronted with his guilt. Having been jailed nineteen years for stealing a loaf to feed his hungry children, he is finally released, embittered and hating his fellow men. He has learned to trust no one and to live for himself.

Once released, Valjean's bitterness increases as he meets contempt and rejection. His identification card which marks him as an ex-convict hinders his ability to find employment and lodging. A kindhearted and other-worldly bishop gives him supper and a night's lodging. But during the night, Valjean steals six silver plates and a silver soup ladle—the Bishop's pride and joy. Upon being caught and arrested, Valjean claims the bishop gave him the plates and the ladle.

Brought before the bishop, Valjean is bewildered to hear him order his release. The clergyman not only backs his story, but reaches up to the mantelpiece and picks up a pair of silver candlesticks. "My friend," said the bishop, "before you go away, here are your candlesticks; take them."

Novelists sometimes perceive human nature more accurately than psychiatrists and psychologists. The incident led to profound repentance on the part of Valjean. The next day,

> his knees buckled under him, as if an invisible power overwhelmed him at a blow, with the weight of his bad conscience; he fell exhausted upon a great stone, his hands clenched in his hair, and his face on his knees, and exclaimed: "What a wretch I am!"
>
> Then his heart swelled, and he burst into tears. It was the first time he had wept in nineteen years.
>
> Jean Valjean wept long, he shed hot tears, he wept bitterly, with more weakness than a woman, with more terror than a child.
>
> While he wept, the light grew brighter and brighter in his mind—an extraordinary light, a light transporting and terrible.[10]

Subsequently, Valjean is seen as a changed man, and eventually he becomes the dignified and respected mayor of a distant town. Once repentance takes place, his conscience is fully awakened, and he begins to see with appalling clarity the reality about himself and the world around him.

Once repentance has taken place, guilt is dealt with, and conscience is progressively normalized. It can then function as it was intended to function, furthering the spiritual and emotional health of its owner.

SEVEN

Emotions Befitting an Earthquake

There never was anything considerable brought to pass in the heart or life of any man living... that had not his heart deeply affected by those things. **Jonathan Edwards**

Repentance can be an emotional experience. Firsthand descriptions of this internal earthquake frequently include weeping or other expressions of deep feeling. Even those that don't mention tears describe a sense of being deeply moved, emotionally alive. Afterward, many describe feelings of almost incomprehensible joy and elation. In fact, we can probably say that repentance and the changes that follow just can't happen without involving our emotions.

This aspect of repentance makes many people uncomfortable, however. Many in our culture—especially men—tend to be uneasy around deep emotion. We have a deeply ingrained fear of not being in control. In addition, we are wary of the extent to which emotions can be manipulated.

What then, is the role of emotion in repentance? *Is* it an inevitable part of lasting change? How does it relate to the process of repentance? How does emotion differ from emotionalism and manipulation?

Let me begin this chapter by discussing the basic nature of

emotion and its role in true repentance. I will look at emotionalism and exploitation of emotion in chapter ten.

EMOTION: NATURAL RESPONSE, LEARNED BEHAVIOR

Emotional expression is natural. Our bodies and nervous systems were designed to respond to stimuli with anger, fear, sadness, and so on. But culture and child-rearing practices modify the emotional responses. If emotion is natural, emotional behavior is culturally learned.

Thus, Caucasians describe Latins as maudlin, explosive, overly emotional. Latins describe northern Europeans as cold. Westerners describe Orientals as inscrutable and enigmatic. There is enough truth in these stereotypes to point to differing fashions of emotional expression in different cultures.

It is not that Germans and Scandinavians have no tear ducts, or that Orientals have no feelings, but that each culture teaches its young to modify their bodily responses. Weeping or not weeping under certain conditions, exercising control or giving way to emotional expression, are matters that one can learn.

Gradually one can even learn to feel or not to feel, since the bodily reactions and experiences go hand in hand. You learn according to the way you are reared. You learn so well, that you learn how to experience or not experience what you call *emotions*.

Cultural fashions change, and with them emotional expression. The period of change is sometimes confusing. Many men, for instance, feel caught in changing patterns of how men are supposed to express emotion. Some men are anxious not to appear sexist or patronizing, while others try to play Rambo. How does the "new man" know when to be strong and supportive and when to be "weak" and vulnerable? Is he to pick up his cues from the woman? If so, he has a problem, for women, too, are uncertain about what kind of emotional expression is appropriate.

What is the ideal place of emotion? Ought we all, men and women alike, to express our emotions? When should we express them, and when restrain them? What is their role in the maintenance of emotional health? Is it ever justifiable to play on one another's emotions—and if not, why not? Our culture is confused. No wonder so many of us are confused as well about emotion.

EMOTION AND THE HUMAN BODY

Just what *is* an emotion? What happens to us when surges of rage sweep over us or when we burst into tears?

There are a number of approaches to answering that question. I would like to begin with physiology. Let's suppose you are walking along the sidewalk in the center of a strange city. You're nervous. You have an appointment to meet a friend, and you're not quite sure whether you understood the directions for the rendezvous. You don't seem to be able to find the place, however, and you begin to panic. The appointment is only five minutes away.

Suddenly you see the person you are to meet on the opposite side of the busy street. She is just about to turn a corner, not having seen you. As you step off the sidewalk there is a screech of brakes, and you quickly jump back. The driver screams obscenities at you before the car drives on.

How do you feel?

For the next five minutes you would probably experience various emotions. You were anxious to begin with, then startled, frightened, and probably angry. Bodily changes have taken place. In spite of what the commercial said, your deodorant may no longer be doing a good job. Your pulse rate will be up, perhaps your blood pressure, too. Your hands may be shaking and your palms sweaty. You will be breathing more quickly. You may even feel sick, faint, and dizzy, wishing you could sit down.

Now let me ask a chicken-and-egg question. Is your pulse rate up because you feel upset? Or is "being upset" your way of describing your experience of the physical changes in your body? Physiologists would say the latter. For them, the sensation of fast breathing, sweat, and accelerated heartbeat *is* anxiety. I am inclined to agree. What we call fear, anger, or depression is a combination of bodily reactions which we interpret as emotion.

However, a more important question lies beneath either approach. Why do bodily changes occur when brakes squeal and car drivers shout nasty obscenities at you?

W.B. Cannon was perhaps the greatest American physiologist of the twentieth century. All the work of later researchers such as Hans Selye builds on the groundwork of Cannon's original investigations. One of his most popular books was entitled *The Wisdom of the Body*.

Cannon's studies made it clear that the emotions we experience and the bodily changes that accompany them are for our benefit. When we are angry and frightened, our bodies are being readied for "fight or flight." Our pulse rate and blood pressure go up. Blood is diverted from those areas of our body where it serves routine operations (such as digestion) and rushed to brain and muscle, where it might be needed to cope with a crisis. This is the way the body readies us for rapid thought and physical action. We are all set to handle an emergency—like a leap back to the sidewalk.

These bodily mechanisms were more useful in days gone by. Had we lived at a time when a tiger or a sword-bearing warrior might leap upon us unexpectedly, our muscles would be instantly ready, and our brains would be unusually clear. Our chances of survival would increase.

Your sidewalk incident is different, however. Aside from your leap back to the curb, the situation does not call for quite the same sort of action. The car does not wave a sword at you. Instead you are stuck with angry feelings about the driver's insults. The feelings have no natural outlet. Your blood pressure and pulse rate stay up for a while, your body remaining on the alert, ready to meet a tiger or a sword-bearing warrior. But neither are likely to appear.

Your angry driver, on the other hand, may be smiling and saying, "I told that stupid idiot where to get off!" Like you, he was at first frightened and then angry, but his outburst—plus the sight of your panic—may have relieved him, releasing some of his tension, and leaving him calmer.

Cannon made many points in his work, two of the most important being the two we have been looking at:

First, our bodies are designed to react to emergencies. The emotions we experience are merely our awareness of the physiological changes taking place to enable us to handle the emergency.

Second, in the unnatural circumstances of the late twentieth century, we are often readied for actions we cannot take. You can do nothing to the driver who just insulted you, and your friend on the other side of the street may disappear while you are still staring angrily at the rear of the car. And with the excessive stimulation, the overdose of perceptual input from every side, we grow weary, overstimulated, no longer able to respond with enthusiasm to anything.

We are now in a better position to understand why repentance can involve strong emotional responses. In chapter three we saw that the greatest threat to the infant human being is the threat of abandonment. René Spitz's discoveries, along with those of the Harlows, teach us two things. First, infants perceive love largely in terms of touch. Second, Spitz's work suggests that in human infants (as distinct from monkeys), the touch has to be the touch of a special person.

All our lives (whether we know it or not) we fear abandonment, but yet crave the special touch of the Supreme Parent. Augustine perceived this. In the very first book of his

Confessions he makes the famous statement, "… you have made us for yourself, and our hearts are restless until they can find peace in you."[1]

At a very deep level in our minds an association exists between God and one of our parents. The dread and the fear of God are the dread and fear of parent, the dread and fear of punishment, of abandonment. The longing for the divine caress is the longing for the soothing touch of a parent.

All of us stand naked before a vast and terrifying universe. Either we shut the terror out of our minds, adapting the universe to our puny needs, or else we cry, "Who are you, Father-Mother? And where?"

Our problem is linked with our early experiences of our parents (many long since forgotten). I have known Christian women tell me, "I can relate to the idea of Jesus, but not God the father." Always in those cases I have found a history of fear of their human father.

Repentance faces us with these issues. We see our sin and failure as we have never seen them before. Terror of divine abandonment arises, with all the physical reactions of terror. Or at the touch of a supernatural hand, we are overwhelmed with relief; then as our terrified sobs subside, our bodies relax and joy supervenes.

EMOTION AND HEALTH

Based on Cannon's research about emotions, we can make some observations that relate to emotion, repentance, and change.

The first observation I would make is that emotion is essentially a healthy mechanism, designed to protect us. Avoiding emotion, in fact, can actually be physically harmful. The hazards of repressed or buried emotion are well known and well documented, especially as they relate to grief. Researchers have gathered ample evidence that those who repress their grief in the face of loss may face serious, even life-threatening depression. Others who fail to face their inner anxiety suffer rising blood pressure and coronary artery disease. Even duodenal ulcers seem related to fear of abandonment and loss of approval.

In addition, both facing, and, in some cases, releasing emotion can counteract the same dangerous tendencies. Norman Cousins has been a well-known exponent of the body's amazing recuperative powers if we work with it rather than ignore its wisdom. Certain relaxation techniques, if regularly practiced, can lower the blood pressure of so-called type A persons. Learning to come to terms with one's fear of disapproval can reduce duodenal symptoms. Getting in touch with repressed grief and beginning to express it can ameliorate and even heal certain types of depression. Even weeping itself can promote mental health.

A group of psychiatric researchers at Yale published an article in a major psychiatric journal describing the health benefits of ritual religious weeping.[2] They examined members of a Caribbean Baptist church who attended a special service designed to let them weep for their sins. The researchers applied specific psychological tests both before and following the service. Their conclusion? "The mourners showed significant improvement on the self-report scales."

EMOTION, REALITY, AND INSANITY

The second observation about emotion that can be derived from Cannon's study is that healthy emotion reflects reality. In a way, it reflects reality more accurately—and more immediately—than intellect does. That is to say, when danger presents itself, our body responds to the real danger we perceive, and it often responds more quickly and more accurately than our minds do.

This point may be obvious, but it is important. We may

know a situation is perilous. But if we do not feel a chill of terror, we may be too slow to act. An intellectual grasp of a situation may not be enough. There are times when we need a quickened pulse—a deep emotion—to help us face and recognize reality. That is one reason deep repentance is almost always connected with deep emotion.

My third observation may initially seem to contradict the first: Insanity—and, you will remember, we are all a bit insane—can mess up the mechanisms governing emotional response. A psychotically depressed man may not care that a truck is about to hit him; he may even want it to. A seriously schizophrenic patient may giggle happily as she cuts her baby in pieces. One severely mentally deficient patient I read about chopped his brother's head off because he "wanted to see his brother's expression when he woke up and found he didn't have his head on any more!"

These are extreme examples, of course, but they illustrate what can happen when we get cut off from reality. If healthy repentance brings us back to reality, repentance therefore can *restore* our out-of-whack emotional response. This is another reason why emotion accompanies repentance.

REPENTANCE AND PSYCHOSIS

Repentance can thus put your feet on a new pathway. It can even cure a psychotic illness. During my early training I saw this happen to the first psychiatric patient in whom I witnessed the repentance factor. No high pressured brain washing from a skilled evangelist affected him—nor even from a half-skilled psychiatrist. I was only a second year resident at the time and I had forgotten any psychiatric skills I may have learned in a few seconds of indignation. Then, before I knew what was happening, the miracle was taking place in front of me. I have described it before.

This miracle took place in a forty-year-old bachelor who had already spent several weeks on the psychiatric ward of a general hospital. He believed he had cancer and that we were lying to him when we told him he showed no evidence of it. He had no energy, no appetite and he couldn't sleep. He was given antipsychotic pills and anti-depressant pills, all of which left him unchanged. So we gave him ten electro-convulsive treatments. Still no change. Treatment showed not the slightest sign that it would ever work.

I had him in my office to try to get a better handle on what could be wrong. He talked about earlier years in his life, telling me two matters still troubled him. He had drunk a bottle of beer years before in defiance of his doctor's orders. More significantly, he had avoided enlistment in World War II, and felt guilty because some of his friends had died in Europe. Curiously, he felt equally bad about both his "sins." He was experiencing "survivors' guilt," and experiencing it in an abnormal degree over too long a period.

As we talked, something mysterious happened. An invisible door swung open between us so that our naked spirits faced each other. "What about forgiveness?" I asked him.

"I want it so *bad*."

"What's your religion?"

"Russian Orthodox."

"And what does your priest say about how you can be forgiven?"

"He doesn't talk too much. We go to confession."

"And what does that do?"

"I don't often go."

I groped for words. "But if you did go, why would God forgive you?"

"Because Christ died. He shed blood."

"*So?*"

"But I'm too bad for that."

Unaccountably I grew angry. No logical reason. It just

132 / Changing on the Inside

happened. "What d'you mean you're too bad?"

His voice was rising like my own. "I don't deserve to be forgiven."

"You're darn right you don't!" He looked up at me surprised. "I can't be a hypocrite. I gotta make amends."

It may be hard to believe, but I found my anger increasing. "And who d'you think you are to say Christ's death was not good enough for you? Who are you to feel you must add your miserable pittance to the great gift God offers you? Is his sacrifice not good enough for the likes of you?"

We continued to stare at each other, and suddenly he began both to cry and to pray at once. I wish I could remember his exact words. There's something indescribably refreshing about the first real prayer a man prays, especially when he doesn't know proper prayer-talk. As nearly as I can recall, he said something like this: "God, I didn't know. I'm real sorry. I apologize—I didn't mean to offend you." More sobs, tears, running nose. I passed him a box of Kleenex. "God, thank you.... It's amazing... I didn't know it worked like that. Gee, God, I don't know how to say it. Thank you. Thanks an awful lot. Gee, God, thank you."

I prayed, my normal fluency a little hampered by the patient's emotion, while he mopped his face with Kleenex.

His eyes were shining and he shook my hand. "Thanks Doc. Thanks a lot. How come nobody ever told me before?"

We cut out all medication. During the following week I did little more than bid him, "Good morning, how are you?" each day. I wanted to let others record his progress. And they did. The notes on his chart read, "Remarkable improvement. No longer seems depressed. Paranoid ideation not expressed. Making realistic plans for future."

Then one day he said, "Doc, I know you're busy. I just gotta talk to you." As soon as we sat down he started. "I don't know how to say it Doc, but it's like I've been blind all my life and now—well, now I can see." He had never read a Bible, never sung a hymn with that kind of language in it.

Yet he was almost quoting verbatim.

Carefully I checked his mental status as we talked. No depression. No sign of mania. Paranoid thinking and nihilistic delusions—only the barest trace. He was practically made whole.[3]

This man had repented. Not of his two "sins." He had been repenting of them for months. Repentance is not so much *feeling sorry*—but experiencing a revolution in your understanding of reality. Faced with my indignation, he had suddenly realized his real offense had been to despise God's mercy in Christ. Instantly, he had changed. He also acknowledged his wrong attitude to God. The change had been followed by other changes and releases. Within a week his psychotic depression had evaporated.

The repentance produced great good. My patient had participated "in the results of an action initiated by another." His participation had put his feet on a helpful pathway, the pathway of vastly improved mental health. He had accepted what for him was a startling new reality, and it transformed his clinical condition. We were all agreed on this—the senior staff physician, the social worker, the psychologist, all the nurses, and me. When he left the hospital he was thoroughly well.

I do not suggest for a moment that repentance should be the standard form of treatment for psychotic states. Certainly the experience of repentance always moves us in the direction of reality, since it springs from a vision of it and an acceptance of it. Rather I am suggesting that where the absence of repentance creates a psychosis (as it sometimes does), then repentance will cure the psychosis.

EMOTION AS A MOTIVATING FACTOR

A fourth important observation is that emotion provides motivation for us to act on what we know.

One of the big problems in life is that things we consciously believe do not always seem real to us. We may "know" it is dangerous to drive too fast, and still screech madly around the curves. We may "believe" we should eat less, but still feel we can get away with just a *little* ice cream—and then just a little more. Diabetics may know that sitting down with a box of chocolates is deadly for them, but they still do it.

More serious, a father may know his anger is destroying his relationships with other members of the family—indeed, it is destroying them—yet continue to explode. He may say, "I know it's wrong. I ought not to do it." But his outbursts continue. He prays about it, sees a counselor about it, determines never to do it again—but does it.

In each case, the intellectual realization of the reality is inadequate. To use an AA expression, these people "have not hit bottom" yet. Their wills are paralyzed because they are not sufficiently in touch with reality.

Their emotions are one way to connect them to the reality of what they think or believe and to motivate them to act.

The idea that some people's actions are psychologically uncontrollable has been incorporated into law in some of the United States. In those states, an offender may go free if the lawyer can prove that he or she was the subject of "an uncontrollable urge"—even an urge to kill someone. In law-school discussions of such laws, a hypothetical, legal test of "uncontrollability" has arisen: Could the urge to kill have been controlled in a different circumstance—for instance, if the killer had the state police at his elbow at the time of the impulse? Having a policeman at your elbow has a powerful emotional effect under certain circumstances; the impulse you could not resist a moment before, you can now resist with ease. To raise such a question could be called the "policeman at the elbow" test. Terror, like other emotions, motivates.

This, in turn, sheds light on how we can face our strange

inability to do things we know we *must* do, and avoid doing what we know we ought not to do. Part of the answer is: we get emotionally involved, and the emotion motivates us.

THE FAILURE OF WESTERN EDUCATION

One way of viewing the complex relationship between what we know and what we are motivated to do uses the time-tested descriptive categories of head and heart, intellect and emotion. Some people tend to rely primarily on the head to guide their decisions; others follow their heart.

Yet an overdependence on either head or heart is mistaken. A human being is neither all intellect nor all emotion. Both are essential to our humanity. Both are part of the way God created us.

The ancients knew that true learning, true wisdom involves both head learning and heart learning. Western society, however, has long emphasized abstract conceptual knowledge over intuitive or emotional knowledge. This has tended to isolate us from the wisdom of our emotions. I believe it has also tended to cut us off from a healthy view of reality.

Our educational systems perpetuate this unbalanced approach to reality. Even in the practical sciences students are taught to adopt a godlike attitude as they investigate the universe around us. True, they are taught they are merely a part of that same universe—marvelously complex organisms involved in the totality of the cosmos. But the admission is a token admission since the whole method of study represents its denial. We investigate as though we were aliens, separated from what we investigate. As a result, we tend to be cut off from our very selves.

As long as education overemphasizes an intellectual acquiring of concepts and neglects the totality of the human organism, the knowledge imparted by the system will be spurious—or at best incomplete. As a result, we have a society that in a sense is insane, cut off from reality. Even religious educational institutions fall into the trap. Jealous of their academic standing, they kowtow to the system as a whole, sending cerebrally polished but spiritually impoverished men and women to lead churches and synagogues.

FAITH AND THE EMOTIONS

There is a faith which is a faith in the head, and another which involves both the head and the heart. Only the latter, which sometimes involves deep emotion, is genuine. The Welsh Christians wept as they realized their sin.

In my own experience, the tears come not over my sins—although I have mourned them deeply—but at the deep assurances of the Lord's love that come after I confess my sins. Remember, it is not God's severity that leads us to repentance, but his kindness (see Rom 2:4). As I grasp once more, that in spite of my sin, in spite of my being such a creep, God really does love me, I am often moved to tears.

Jonathan Edwards, the great Puritan preacher (later president of Harvard University) pinpointed the vital role of emotion in faith in the sentence I quoted at the head of this chapter: "There never was anything considerable brought to pass in the heart or life of any man living... that had not his heart deeply affected by those things."[4]

What Edwards called affections we now call emotions. *Deeply affected*, in his language, means profoundly moved. On the same page he writes, "Nothing is more manifest... than that the things of religion take hold of men's souls no further than they *affect* them."

Nothing is more obvious, in other words, than that any religious faith is meaningless that does not involve profound emotional impact. This does not mean that religious people must remain constantly in the throes of emotional expression. I certainly don't equate faith with being emotionally out of control! Faith must include head as well as heart. But a faith that does not at some point touch the one who professes it at a deep, emotional level is a faith I would seriously question.

GETTING HEAD AND HEART TOGETHER

In ancient Hebrew thought, the heart was usually considered to be the center of feeling-action. The distinction between head knowledge and heart knowledge which I am making does not seem to have been an issue. All knowledge was one. And it will be if head and heart can get together. In the balance between what head knows and what "heart" perceives lies the true secret of motivation. The two must come together.

Ancient Christian writers picked up the importance of heart from the ancient Hebrews. Later Christian writers, sensing the distinction between head grasp and heart grasp, began to discuss the distinction between the two, and the desirability of their connection. Richard Baxter, a seventeenth century Puritan writes: "*Consideration* (a word he seemed to use almost synonymously with *meditation*) as it were, opens the door between the head and the heart."[5] For Baxter, and for many ancient writers, meditation provided the key for connecting our understanding with our feelings and thus our behavior.

Baxter says: "As digestion turns food into chyle and blood for vigorous health, so meditation turns the truths received and remembered into warm affection, firm resolution, and holy conversation."[6] To put Baxter's assertion into more modern language, *meditation arouses feeling and thus motivates action*.

But what is meditation? Meditation is the deliberate, disciplined practice of focusing our attention on a truth or an aspect of reality—ideally, on the truth of the loving presence of Christ in and with us. Meditation consists of dwelling on reality, and God in me *is* reality.

In some sense, God is in every human being that lives. He may not always be present in saving and redeeming power. But his presence maintains heartbeats, keeps blood flowing freely, and supports second by second the molecular substructure of every nerve impulse. You would be dead in seconds if it were not for the sustaining presence and power of God in and around your body. And as he watches and controls, he also loves tenderly.

Much of the time, however, we do not live in the moment by moment experience of God's power or love. We do not live in reality at all. Our attention is elsewhere. So alien does such an idea seem that we shake our heads unbelievingly. We live in a world made up of our own notions. A dozen half-baked philosophies jingle in confusion in our heads, along with fantasies, hopes, fears, worries, and half-remembered videos and TV programs.

Meditation offers us an opportunity, in the midst of our distractions, to reconnect with reality and the emotions that are a part of that reality. For Christians it ought to be the third leg in the three-legged stool of Bible study, prayer, and meditation. Prayer for most of us means talking to God. Meditation means reflecting on truth, letting it sink in. Meditation involves silent musing. Without any one of the three, the stool is of limited usefulness. And the one most people avoid is meditation—taking time daily to sit and ponder what is real.

Meditation has changed my life. Or to put it more accurately, God has changed me as I have learned to meditate. Through the discipline of setting aside regular time to contemplate reality, my heart has been ignited, my spirit stirred, my hangups released, and my behavior revolutionized. As I have waited silently before the God who is active in the world, and also inside me, as I have struggled to wake up to the fact that he cares for me right now—I have been changed. God has turned the "truths received and remembered" into "warm affection, firm resolution, and holy conversation."

But I have paid a price. I have paid it in time, in discipline, in sleeplessness, in discouragement when I found meditation a difficult skill to acquire. But I do not regret paying the price. My regret is that I have meditated too little and too late. What is our time worth—and, for that matter, life itself—if at the end of it we enter the great beyond beggared and naked? For the only things we will be able to take with us from this life are those things that have value in an economy based on holiness and love.

I shall say more about meditation in chapter nine. However, meditation is not the only way our feelings are stirred and our motivation aroused. An experiential encounter with painful reality can do the same. The prodigal son, for example, probably felt both moved and motivated as he sat among the pigs, contrasting his current lot with what he had once enjoyed. And these emotions certainly motivated. At last, feelings stirred and will set in motion, homeward he went!

Chuck Colson had yet a different experience. His host did the meditating for Chuck as he read to him. And in the darkness God took the initiative and began to stir Chuck's emotions until repentance took place. Often, especially in times of great revival, God stirs people's hearts directly. The reading of a book may set it off. Or a sermon in a synagogue or church might do so.

THE HEALTHY RELEASE OF GROUP EMOTION

No right thinking person favors the manipulation of mass emotion. We have seen too much of it. Unprincipled rabble-rousers, both religious and political, have caused too much damage in the past.

Yet there are ways in which good leaders can mobilize

healthy emotional responses both in small groups and in nations. Psychology and psychiatry continually explore ways of doing it in group psychotherapy. During World War II, Winston Churchill mobilized the resolve of the British nation with his words, "We will fight them on the beaches...." I suspect that factors beyond mere oratory power account for the astonishing results of well-directed words. But whatever they may be, the results can be profoundly healthful.

More than two hundred years ago in New England, Jonathan Edwards preached a sermon entitled "Sinners in the Hands of an Angry God." The sermon is stirring enough, but Edwards was not a particularly stirring orator. He read his sermon by candlelight from a handwritten manuscript. He was short-sighted and had to peer at his handwriting closely. His voice was high-pitched and not particularly compelling. Altogether a lot was working against Edwards when he preached about God's anger.

Nevertheless supernatural factors were operating in the building that night to bring about repentance. Panic broke out in the church. People wept for their sins. Men and women found themselves clinging to the pillars that supported the roof, feeling the ground beneath their feet was too treacherous to prevent their feet from sliding into hell. And the changes that took place in their lives were the first wave of the massive American revival known as the Great Awakening.

The first record of such group repentance is found in the Hebrew Scriptures, in the book of Nehemiah. Nehemiah was a governor of Jerusalem at a time when Jews were returning to Jerusalem after having been captives in foreign countries. Nehemiah 8 describes a gathering of the people of Jerusalem round one of the city gates. They have come to hear a reading from the Law, a reading they themselves had requested. There under an open sky they listen for several hours.

The reading is not in itself dramatic or exciting. Try reading the Book of Leviticus in the Old Testament—hardly light entertainment. That may have been one of the books being read.

Now, think for a minute. Picture yourself in an open-air meeting with several thousand people. There is no "entertainment," no loudspeakers. Priests are reading—for hours—from a dry set of law books. There are questions and answers.

Under such circumstances, would Bible books like Numbers and Leviticus move you deeply? Yet because the Holy Spirit was active, this is precisely what happened. The crowd wept. They wept so much that Nehemiah the governor, Ezra the priest, and other leaders broke up the meeting, moving among the people and telling them to rejoice rather than weep.

What was happening? Evidently it had become vividly clear to those Jews who had gathered that they had failed God badly. They evidently saw the appalling and unforgivable gap between their behavior and God's requirements as his special people.

However, Nehemiah and Ezra saw matters in a better light. To them, the fact that the truth had come home to everyone was good news rather than bad. The people were facing reality. Now they knew what the divine requirements were; their eyes had been opened to the reality of God and of themselves. It was time to celebrate as well as weep. And celebrate they did (Neh 8:10-12), prior to one of the most important reforms in Jewish history. That reform so set the character of the Jewish identity that the Hebrews were able to weather internal conflict and foreign invasion for four hundred more years.

EMOTION AND OUR RESPONSE TO GOD

I insist again that emotion must correspond to reality. There is no point in leaping in panic to the sidewalk if you are not in danger. Fear is for danger, grief for suffering, joy to strengthen us as we grasp the nature of good. Such appropriate emotions are a sign of health, a sign that our personalities are integrated and we are in touch with reality.

The heart of reality for each person lies in his or her relationship with the Creator of all of us. Each of us has a relationship which falls into one of three categories.

Some of us have our backs to God and are moving ever further from him. If we belong to that group, we may or may not have any interest in him. Others of us are searching for God. Still others have a sort of marriage relationship with God and are growing daily in the delight of intimacy with him.

God's attitude to all three groups is in one sense the same. He may be angry toward the first group, but it is the anger of love. He reaches out to the second group in love and tenderness, assuring them that if they ask, they will receive (see Jn 16:24). And the third group he lovingly guides and nourishes, teaching them his way as they continue to grow.

There is a sense in which it is impossible to get away from God. Francis Thompson, a nineteenth-century opium addict, discovered that to be the case. As a result of his encounter with God, he wrote *The Hound of Heaven*, a moving poem about a relentlessly pursuing, loving God.

David the psalmist discovered the same reality:

Where can I go from your Spirit?
Where can I flee from your presence?
If I go up to the heavens, you are there;
if I make my bed in the depths, you are there.
If I say, "Surely the darkness will hide me
and the light become night around me,"
even the darkness will not be dark to you;
the night will shine like the day
for darkness is as light to you.

(Ps 139:7-8, 11-12)

We turn our backs on God only to discover we are facing him. Charles Colson (whether he had thought of it in those terms or not) had turned his back on God in his blind and ruthless pursuit of power. He was mistaken, of course, for power brings no real happiness. Yet in reaching out for that power, he was still really reaching out for happiness. And in reaching out for happiness he was reaching out for God. But he was ignorant of his real longings, and of what his heart really demanded, until God's Spirit began to work on him.

What all of us in each of the three groups must realize is that we yearn for complete and ultimate acceptance. We crave the loving embrace of a Father. It is an embrace we will not find unless and until we can face our own wretchedness and nakedness, our need for forgiveness. When we do face reality, we find that at the heart of reality there is a God who loves us enough to pick us up in our naked wretchedness and to wash and clothe us himself.

Clearly if we are like the people in Hans Christian Andersen's story of "The Emperor Without Clothes" and cannot recognize nakedness when we see it, then we will not know we are naked. In that case we will turn elsewhere for satisfaction. We will be like the pompous emperor, walking through the streets imagining we are clothed, when we are wretched and miserable and blind and naked. But because the crowds around us either fear to discover they are fools or else do not know nakedness when they see it, any more than we do ourselves, our delusion will continue.

If, on the other hand, God shows us our true condition, there will be nothing that moves us to deeper repentance than the awareness of the love of God. And then, emotionally speaking, there will be nothing that moves us more deeply.

THE EMOTIONS OF REPENTANCE

It is no accident that much of the emotion I have described in this chapter involves tears. For tears are a natural response when we are confronted with the loving reality of God and with our own deep inadequacy.

The great evangelist Charles Finney had a vision of Jesus just after he had committed himself to him: "He said nothing, but looked at me in such a manner as to break me right down at his feet.... I wept aloud like a child, and made such confessions as I could with my choked utterance. It seemed to me that I bathed his feet with my tears.... "⁷

Later, Finney grew to understand what had happened. He explains how it works when someone becomes aware of the love of God: "In relation to God, he feels towards sin as it really is, and here is the source of those gushings of sorrow.... When he views it in relation to God, then he weeps; the fountains of his sorrow gush forth, and he wants to get right down on his face and pour out a flood of tears over his sins."⁸

Catholics and Protestants agree about this important truth. Jean LaFrance, a French Jesuit, says, "Discovering your sin is less important than discovering Christ—then you are close to the blessing of tears." He goes on to explain that you "cannot discover [Christ's] face without discovering at the same time what you are rejecting in your heart. This is your real sin."⁹

Weeping is only one of the emotions associated with true repentance, however. Peace, gentleness, and a greater longing to forgive others may supervene. Joy is just as likely to follow—delirious joy over the wonder of being forgiven, of God's loving acceptance. Earlier we saw that when the Jews wept in horror over their failure to keep the law, Nehemiah and Ezra ran among them telling them to rejoice. The day was a day for celebration, for God's word had come to them again! So they rejoiced and had a party. Tears and laughter are often intertwined when the earthquake of repentance shakes us.

In another book I described the experience of a man I call Joe. Joe had to be disciplined according to the custom of his church, to spend a period outside its fellowship because of his sexual sins. It was a terrible experience for him and included a time of deepening awareness of his corruption. "I thought I had hit rock bottom before, but now I began to see my life riddled with deceit and my heart with sinful disease. The process was a long one."

Joe's despair continued until one day, while standing in an unemployment line, he was struck by the truth about Christ as expressed in a book he was reading. He says, "It hit me like a lightening bolt. I felt elated. I couldn't stop smiling. I thought my heart was going to jump out of my chest. The man behind me must have thought I had gone crazy. As soon as I left the unemployment desk I almost ran to the car, got inside and howled for joy!"[10]

The truth Joe had "seen" was the one aspect of reality he had needed to see in order for his behavior to be transformed. And the emotion he experienced corresponded with that exhilarating truth.

When truth, ultimate truth, breaks over us, it is all the same whether we weep or howl for joy. For myself I still do either from time to time. It is the sanest form of insanity. It is the discovery of wonder and worship. It is the discovery that a Presence I thought I dreaded is the Presence I crave most. Francis Thompson expresses it movingly:

Halts by me that footfall:
Is my gloom, after all,
Shade of his hand, outstretched caressingly?
"Ah, fondest, blindest, weakest,
I am He whom thou seekest!
Thou dravest love from thee, who dravest Me."[11]

EIGHT

Turning Your Own Life Around: Journey Toward Change

A journey of a thousand miles begins with the first step. Mao Tse Tung

If you have read this far, I may have awakened a hope of changing your life in some way. If so, I am very glad. I believe profound change is possible for everyone. However difficult the problem, however resistant to change, however many failures have occurred in the past, radical transformation is possible—and possible for you. In this and the coming chapters, I want to outline a practical strategy for opening your life to that kind of change.

THE LIMITS OF CHANGE

Thus far, I have proposed that the only change worth having is real change, lasting and positive change. I have also said that such change is inextricably tied to facing reality—reality about yourself and about the moral structure of the universe. Your experience of change will depend in part on your vision of reality. And there is a limit as to what you can do about that.

You can open yourself to experience more of reality. You can even write a list of the things you see wrong in yourself—your sins, follies, and weaknesses. But to really see them as God sees them—that is something God himself must show you.

Reality, you may recall, can be very painful. Yet the greater the pain, the more profound the resulting change. The pain of seeing yourself in a less flattering light—as, say, a truly weak or judgmental or cowardly person, a person whom few people would be willing to love—is what holds the potential for change. Let me say it again. Nobody has the natural inclination or capacity to see themselves in this way. There is in all of us a mechanism psychologists call *denial*, by which we protect ourselves from psychic pain. This inherent mechanism has to be overcome in some way in order for change to occur. Overcoming the mechanism of denial must involve some outside impetus. It's no use trying to make yourself repent by developing a new and painful view of yourself or rehearsing your faults. You will only succeed in becoming depressed—and you probably still won't be able to see the real problem.

Vision is something that happens to you, that somebody else does to you. And the Someone who does it best is the Spirit of God.

THE REVEALING PRESENCE

It is true that other people can help you overcome your denial. In the case of Ward Gasque, for instance, it was his doctor who laid out the facts of his danger—the danger of killing himself by his poor eating habits. Others have found that trusted friends or support groups can help them see themselves and reality more clearly.

God, however, opens our eyes far better than doctors or friends or even "fellow strugglers." When we open ourselves to him, consciously or unconsciously, he shows us ourselves in terms that transcend mere death. God enables us to see ourselves in the light of ultimate reality.

But seeing the painful reality about yourself is not all that is needed for change. You also need the sense that you are loved and accepted in spite of the horror of who you really are. Again, other people can help flesh out this transforming acceptance. But the most important Source of this pure love is God.

Only God can see the depth of our shame and still truly love and accept us. Some dim grasp of such an acceptance made Chuck Colson cry, "Take me! Take me!" A similar sense of having grieved Someone who loved them made the Welsh Christians weep in chorus. A sense of God's bountiful love and mercy made Tom want to return the favor by helping people in Africa.

In all these cases, and in many others I could quote, there was also a sense of an invisible presence. It is at this point that you may experience difficulty. You may never have felt this presence in your life. You may not even believe in a God—or you may believe but struggle to see that he is real and active in your life. All I can say is that God is faithful. If you persist in seeking him—or letting him seek you—God will act in your life. And when you do encounter him, you will have no problem whatever in believing. When God moves in on you, unbelief or indifference ceases to be an option.

My personal physician was talking about this the other day, and I got him to write down what he told me. Originally a top-notch geology student, he "knew" that evolution excluded the possibility of a Creator. An experience of God as he sat in the woods one day changed all that in moments. He remembers:

> "At that moment I experienced two things.
> "It was as though a light went on in the shadows of my mind; like a long-missing piece of jigsaw puzzle was found. God was!... My mind was renewed. My world view shifted. I believed.
> "Secondly, with me in that forest was a Presence. I was in the quiet of the forest, but I was not alone. Even today as I recollect the event, I may experience tingles shooting along my spine. I sensed physically God with me.... Upon my return to camp my life was different."

I could suggest any number of psychological explanations of my doctor's experience. However a hard fact remains: he was never the same again. His career changed, his life remains changed. People who come face to face with God are changed for ever.

HELPING YOURSELF CHANGE

But "lightning bolt" moments like that don't happen to everyone—not even to Christians. God alone knows the reason for this. Each of us is different and repentance comes to us in different ways.

One reason change may be slow in coming, however, is that at some level we are not yet ready for it or are even resisting it. Remember, repentance is in essence a decision—a response to the work of the Holy Spirit. It is a decision we can make unconsciously, but it is a decision nevertheless. Until we are ready to respond to the Spirit's prompting, therefore, deep change will not happen in our lives.

We cannot determine when or why God will move in our lives. But there is a way we can prepare ourselves to respond. A very practical and helpful guide to opening our lives to repentance and then living a life of ongoing positive change can be found in the Twelve Steps commonly used by Alcoholics Anonymous and its sister groups.

As I have discussed earlier, many Christians are highly critical of Twelve Step programs, and I myself have some reservations about their approach to reality. However, I believe their basic approach is both sound and helpful in enabling change. With some modifications, I believe the Twelve Steps can be an important key in helping you turn your life around and staying on a healthy path.

Before I look at the Twelve Steps in more detail, however, I want to look briefly at some of the criticisms of others and some of my own reservations about the AA approach.

First, I believe Christian criticism of AA has a sour grapes quality. Christians have been doing a little more in recent years for alcoholics than formerly, but we have a long way to go before we catch up with what AA and its sister programs have done to help people change for the better. For many years, most of us Christians drew our righteous skirts about us and regarded alcoholics as unworthy of our gospel efforts.

The Salvation Army is an exception. They and a few downtown missions and outreach efforts have gotten involved. But the rest of us, when we discovered that the gospel we preached did not seem to deliver alcoholics, concluded that the alcoholics were at fault. Evidently, they just didn't want what we had to offer. If AA did help them, then it could not have much to do with the real gospel.

There were several things wrong with our attitude and our conclusions. For one thing, we lacked the quality that most characterized Jesus—compassion for the lost and the suffering. We turned our backs on lushes, and later on drug addicts and gays. (We had always avoided prostitutes.)

Our second error was getting caught up in running an institution rather than living the gospel. Protestants and

Catholics alike failed at this point. While recovering alcoholics reached out to fellow strugglers, we kept ourselves busy with churchly concerns.

We also assumed that we understood the gospel, when we understood only a part of it. We criticized one another's view of repentance. Protestants pointed out (I believe correctly) that some Catholics confused penance and repentance. But Protestants largely failed to preach repentance in our concern with stressing faith in Christ alone. We failed to see that saving faith in Christ can only arise in repentant hearts.

With these failures in mind, I want to take a second look at the Twelve Steps that are the heart of the AA recovery program. All of them reflect biblical teaching. Some reflect biblical teaching Christians are in danger of forgetting and rarely practice. Nevertheless, I believe they are incomplete Bible teaching, and at one point they are seriously watered down.

The founders of AA knew this. They were not pretending to invent what are actually very ancient principles. But they also knew who they were trying to reach—men and women for whom the very word *God* had bitter associations, who resented certain people who quoted God while at the same time shunning them.

As I have said, I believe the decision made by AA may have been mistaken. I would certainly modify some of the Twelve Steps. But I cannot be too critical. What is my track record for helping people change?

God has used AA and its sister organizations to rescue countless folks who would have otherwise been lost forever. After all, he is the source of truth, and truth, even incomplete truth, changes people. Why else are we Christians so effective at points where AA is not?

The mistake we all make is to assume that we, perhaps we alone, grasp the whole truth. None of us do. Our minds and spirits are not large enough.

The timing of God's intervention and even the manner of

it will vary from person to person. Your earthquake could be violent or very gentle, the emotions tumultuous or relatively gentle. Or, as one person put it, you may wake up one morning and "realize the topography's changed. You don't recall the rumble, but there's a mountain here." What matters, however it happens, is the change in you that can take place.

Having laid this foundation, then, let's take a look at how a modified version of the Twelve Steps can open our lives to the real and positive changes God wants to make in us. Steps 1 through 7 involve the process of repentance, at least your own part in it. Steps 8 to 10 have more to do with on-going, life-long repentance.

AA'S TWELVE STEPS TOWARD RECOVERY FROM AL-COHOLISM[1]

1. We admitted we were powerless over alcohol—that our lives had become unmanageable.

2. Came to believe that a Power greater than ourselves could restore us to sanity.

3. Made a decision to turn our will and our lives over to the care of God *as we understood Him.*

4. Made a searching and fearless moral inventory of ourselves.

5. Admitted to God, to ourselves, and to another human being the exact nature of our wrongs.

6. Were entirely ready to have God remove all these defects of character.

7. Humbly asked Him to remove all our shortcomings.

8. Made a list of all persons we had harmed, and became willing to make amends to them all.

9. Made direct amends to such people wherever possible, except when to do so would injure them or others.

10. Continued to take personal inventory and when we were wrong promptly admitted it.

11. Sought through prayer and meditation to improve our conscious contact with God *as we understood Him,* praying only for knowledge of his will for us and the power to carry that out.

12. Having had a spiritual awakening as the result of these steps, we tried to carry this message to alcoholics, and to practice these principles in all of our affairs.

STEPS 1 AND 2: ENTRY INTO HELPLESSNESS

Steps 1 and 2 of AA's program involve the alcoholic's recognition of total helplessness over alcohol, as well as over life generally, and the willingness for a greater Power to take over.

In a similar sense, moving toward lasting change must begin with the recognition that no amount of resolution on your part can bring it about. For repentance to take place, remember, we need to *see* something—and more than just intellectually. We need to see by divine illumination. We can't make it happen. The first step toward real and lasting change, therefore, is to admit our helplessness.

For this reason, and in order to keep the "steps" parallel with AA's, I have lumped steps 1 and 2 together. You take both in preparing to repent, when you cry out to God to show you what you can never see otherwise.

There are two kinds of change for the better—reformation by effort of the will, and the change wrought by a Power greater than ourselves. So long as you can manage by your own efforts, the change will be relatively superficial. So long as you can get by on your own efforts, you will never really change. Only your outward behavior (and sometimes not even that) is changing when you believe you can change yourself. You act a part that is not really you. Because your inner being never changes, your behavioral changes will most likely be short-lived.

What makes you ready to take this first step of admitting powerlessness? You reach a point that alcoholics call "hitting bottom." When you hit bottom, you see for the first time that you haven't a hope of making it on your own. Only at that point are you ready to receive the help of a "Power greater than" yourself. As long as you entertain any hope whatever that you can learn how to change yourself, you will trust yourself rather than Someone greater than you.

You can think you have hit bottom before you really have. Many, perhaps most struggling alcoholics take several cracks at "working the steps." They begin before they truly hit bottom. Many alcoholics who face step 1—which in a sense is a confession of hitting bottom—still entertain the unconscious hope of making it on their own.

They may say, and really feel, that they know they are helpless. But hope dies hard. It is hard to stop longing for the strength to "make it" on our own. The moment many alcoholics begin to make headway, they begin to feel a little cocky, a little more sure of themselves. This psychological condition undermines their relationship with any Power greater than themselves. So they begin to drink again, sure they can stop after "just one." Soon they take another tumble. Then, after a few binges, they may be ready for Step 1 again.

To hit bottom means to know—really know, in the depth of your being—that your case is hopeless and there really is nothing you can do about your condition. This is the point— at the bottom—where life begins. This is what a life of repentance is all about.

When Jesus picked the twelve apostles, he did not select men for their superior qualities. He told them frankly that without him they were helpless. He says the same of all of us. "Apart from me," he said, "you can do nothing" (Jn 15:5).

The fact of the matter is that we are indeed helpless. But to experience that powerlessness, to know in the depth of our being that we are helpless, is another matter. But God is willing to come to our aid even there. He is willing to show us our helplessness, not only in words, but through our experiences. God may do it the slow way, through the normal circumstances of life, or the fast way, by the illumination of the Holy Spirit. Or he may show us by a combination of the two, as in the case of Chuck Colson.

If we ask him, then in one way or another, God will do it. He certainly will. Therefore we tell him, that whether we understand the depths of what we are saying, or not, we acknowledge our helplessness. We ask him in his own time and way to deal with us, and for the present to take our words seriously. When we do that, God begins to move in on us, whether we perceive it or not. Sooner or later we will begin to see. Sooner or later his own nature begins to be infused with ours.

Curiously, when this happens, you do not become less yourself, but more yourself. That strength and beauty which is uniquely yours, planned from before creation, begins to shine more clearly. You share a family likeness because God is the original source of your being. Once the separation is gone from between you, he can restore what you had lost.

But first, you need to see this. You need to see that you need to see. You need to cry out for divine illumination. That's what step 1 is all about: *I face the fact, and tell God I now know that I am helpless. I tell him I need to see clearly.*

STEPS 1 AND 2: ASKING FOR HELP

The other side of admitting our helplessness to God is asking for his help. I remember quite clearly when I took that step myself. One day quite a few years ago, driving through the Canadian countryside, I realized I had what in religious language would be called a *heart of stone*—cold, hard, uncaring.

I was fairly well known as a Christian. I knew a bit about

theology and felt that I was balanced in my approach to religious questions. God had even used me to bring many other people to himself. Somehow, however, I had slowly drifted into cynicism and disillusionment, and I had no desire to be different—although I knew I ought to be. Intellectually I had no doubts about God's existence, nor of the many kindnesses he had shown me. It was simply that I had lost interest and stopped caring. I was bored with Christianity.

I tried to express my feelings in a prayer (recorded later in my journal), although I was a little shocked at what I found myself praying.

"I don't love You," I cried aloud. "I don't love anyone else either. I'm only interested in myself. And—though it sounds shocking to say it—I don't care! In fact as I consult my feelings, I couldn't care less!

"Yet I recognize this to be wrong. So I ask you to change me—to give me a heart of flesh in place of this stony heart. I regret what has happened, even though I don't experience any feelings of sorrow. I acknowledge that it is my own fault. I feel as though I am pronouncing empty words—but answer me according to the words."

Weeks passed. Then one day—and I could never remember when the change began—the heart of stone was gone. I loved and I cared—passionately. God had taken my prayer seriously, insincere though it may have seemed. Looking back, I could see that the passionate feelings had been there all along—but buried beneath an accumulation of guilt and fear. As I saw with clearer eyes the love of God toward me, I wept.

I record my own experience to illustrate the fact that we deal with a God who will take your words seriously. He only demands of us that we be as honest with him and with ourselves as we are capable of being. Therefore if you despair, tell him so. If you couldn't care less, tell him so—but tell him also that you want to change and ask his help in doing so. If you are honest and serious, he will take your words at their face value. And change will start.

I suppose that when I confessed to God the hardness of my heart, I had hit bottom in some sense. I had admitted my cynical pride and my self-sufficiency and had acknowledged that I could not even change that. It seems to me in retrospect to have been a bottom below bottom, the starting place for this process of repentance.

Step 1 and 2 then, can be rephrased in this way: *I tell God I need to see my own inner nature as well as his greatness and his kindness. I accept his promise to show me all I need to see.*

STEP 3: AN ACT OF WORSHIP

AA's step 3 is "We made a decision to turn our lives over to God *as we understood him.*"

It is at this point that I depart most radically from the AA program. It makes obvious sense to "turn your life over" to God if you can't cope with life yourself. Yet while I fully understand and appreciate the reasons for "God as we understood him," I find such a God grossly inadequate.

If you turn your life over to your own concept of God, how do you know whether that concept is powerful enough? To help me, God has to be more than a concept. After all, our concepts are limited by our ability to conceive. Even while praying to "God as we understand him," we could still be trying to pull ourselves up "by our own bootstraps." I believe this fact accounts for at least some of AA's failures (although I do not forget their huge successes.) No, if I am to turn my life over to a God, it must be God *as he is.* Not God as I conceive him, but God as he conceives himself to be. If there is a God, then he is a person, not an idea. He is not something I have made up out of my own understanding.

I know, of course, as my friend Betty puts it, that God sometimes "runs with whatever you give him." In her case, he used her reluctant acceptance of the AA phrase to show himself to her, just as he used my grudging prayer to change my heart.

God is merciful. He understands our limited concepts. But I'd rather face at the outset the fact that he is real, not imaginary, and that he has the right to do with me whatever he chooses. I am not into "psyching" myself into a belief in a God of my own creating.

If God is God, then he must by that definition be an object of worship and sacrifice. The apostle Paul writes, "Therefore, I urge you, brothers, in view of God's mercy, to offer your bodies as living sacrifices, holy and pleasing to God—this is your spiritual act of worship" (Rom 12:1).

Given that God is an object worthy of worship and sacrifice, and given that I turn my life over to him in that way (and not merely to get him to help me), then it makes sense that my life will change. In his kindness, and in view of my ignorance, God may let me get by with less. Nevertheless, it is better to "start right" and approach God with a spirit of worship.

With that act of worship comes a promise. Paul goes on to say: "Do not conform any longer to the pattern of this world, but be transformed by the renewing of your mind. Then you will be able to test and approve what God's will is—his good, pleasing and perfect will" (Rom 12:2).

God is interested in renewal, the transformation of our inner beings. He is the one who helps us renew our way of thinking and conceiving. Along this road comes profound change.

Step 3 in working toward repentance is, therefore: *I offer my body as a living sacrifice to God, and as an act of worship.*

STEP 4: THE "FEARLESS MORAL INVENTORY"

I go along thoroughly with AA's fourth step: "We made a searching and fearless moral inventory of ourselves." I have seen the good it can do. I have a son who has had problems with alcohol and drugs. Several times he has wrestled through step 4 of AA, sitting down and writing a list of his sins and shortcomings. "Fearless moral inventories" are something that almost never happen in Protestant circles these days. Even in Catholic circles, the confessional, which once served that purpose, seems to be used less and less. Counselors in evangelistic circles certainly do not encourage inquirers to talk about their sins in detail. For one thing, the mass processing of converts does not allow the necessary time.

I am convinced that is one reason converts often fail to mature both as persons and in their Christian faith. We are in too much of a hurry to get to the part of the gospel of forgiveness because of Christ's shed blood (the *good* news). We do not want to deal with the pain of unconfessed sins, perhaps because we have never adequately faced the pain of our own.

This step is a truly daunting one. A searching and fearless inventory? Not skimping on anything? Facing the truth about myself, with myself? Writing the words down and reading them over? Putting down details, painful and embarrassing details, of things I did which fill me with shame when I consider them now? That is tough stuff, certainly not for the weak at heart.

God's forgiveness is a fact. But the benefit of that fact increases immeasurably when we experience in full measure the pain and shame of our sins—when we sit and look at those sins, written down on paper in our own handwriting.

I hear people say, "Yes, but God forgets all our sins. So why shouldn't we? What's the point of dwelling on the past?"

We are to forget certain things in life and remember others. We are to dwell on those things God has done for us. Granted, I never think of my sins apart from God's forgiveness of them. However, the remembrance of his forgiveness—*along with all the associated shame and horror of my sin*—increases my sense of thanksgiving immeasurably, so that I cry out my praise to God. Worship and praise arise from the sense of contrast between what I did and what God did, between what I am and what he is.

Therefore my adaptation of Step 4 focuses on opening one's heart to repentance by praying this prayer: *"Search me, O God, and know my heart; test me and know my anxious thoughts. See if there is any offensive way in me, and lead me in the way everlasting"* (Ps 139: 23-24).

After such a prayer I sit down and write out, in the light of what God shows me, the searching and fearless moral inventory AA suggests. I must include not only my misdeeds and shameful attitudes, but also my pains, fears, and anxieties, for God wants to change those also. He is the Great Physician who came to heal. In the words of an old song:

He did not come to judge the world
He did not come to blame
He did not only come to seek
It was to save he came.[2]

I write children's fiction as a hobby. In one of the books I give God the name Changer[3]. It is God's will to change you—if you will let him. But he will only change what you see to be in need of change. That is the real reason for the fourth step. *I pray that God will search my heart. I promise God: "As you do so, I will write down those sins and failures to which you draw my attention."*

STEP 5: THE ACHAN MANEUVER

AA's step 5 runs like this: "We admitted to God, to ourselves, and to another human being the exact nature of our wrongs."

Notice the phrase, *the exact nature of our wrongs.* I call this the *Achan Maneuver,* thinking of an incident in the early history of ancient Israel which took place when Israel first invaded the West Bank territory that is now so hotly contested.⁴ The ancient historical account is found in the book of Joshua.

Following a successful campaign against the walled city of Jericho, the Hebrew army is defeated by the less powerful city of Ai. When their leader, Joshua, inquires of God, he is told that Israel has angered him by ignoring his instructions. God subsequently reveals by lot that a man named Achan is the culprit.

When charged, Achan tells the whole story, without any excuses:

> Then Joshua said to Achan, "My son, give glory to the LORD, the God of Israel, and give him the praise. Tell me what you have done; do not hide it from me." Achan replied, "It is true! I have sinned against the LORD, the God of Israel. *This is what I have done: When I saw in the plunder a beautiful robe from Babylonia, two hundred shekels of silver and a wedge of gold weighing fifty shekels, I coveted them and took them. They are hidden in the ground inside my tent, with the silver underneath.*" (Jos 7:19-21, my emphasis)

We see a naive simplicity about Achan's confession. It reminds me of my two-year-old grandson. "John, why ever did you *do* that?" I hear his father asking. Earnestly John replies, "I *wanted* to, Daddy!" Somehow we have lost the childlike simplicity of knowing and admitting what we really enjoy doing, the lusts that ache in us. Real repentance involves a loss of our fear of being found out, of opening our closets to clearly reveal our hidden skeletons.

There is a terrible down side to this story. Achan was punished severely—put to death by stoning, along with his whole family. And it is the fear of exposure and of punishment that makes the Achan maneuver so difficult for us to face.

However, in our case the punishment has already been meted out, not to us, but to someone who volunteered to take the death sentence for us—Jesus. Yet for most of us, telling another person what we have done wrong is still horrendously difficult—a kind of death in its own way.

In discussing the twelve steps, of course, we are talking not about what God does as repentance takes place, but about what we ourselves do. The Achan Maneuver is tough. To carry it out involves breaking the hard armor of secrecy that protects our dignity and pride. It involves being humbled, facing humiliation. However, a willingness to be thus exposed can precede a glorious knowledge of being free from shame.

The AA confession of wrongdoing is threefold: we confess to God, to ourselves, and to another person.

Confessing to God is the obvious first step. John the Apostle assures us that "If we confess our sins, he is faithful and just and will forgive us our sins and purify us from all unrighteousness. If we claim we have not sinned, we make him out to be a liar and his word has no place in our lives" (1 Jn 1:10).

But confessing to God is not enough. To some people, God seems so remote that it is almost easy to confess to him. That's why we are also advised to confess to ourselves and at least one other person. To confess to ourselves begins to penetrate the armor of self-protection. But for many of us, confessing to another human being is the hardest test of all.

To whom should we choose to confess? It may be easier in a sense to confess a specific sin or weakness to a priest or a pastor—and there are times when we should. But it is probably more effective to confess to a close friend or "fellow struggler." Confessing to a nonprofessional is riskier (priests and pastors, like counselors, are sworn to confidentiality, while a friend might blab). But taking the risk is part of what makes the change process work, though clearly we should not choose a "blabby" friend just to make it tougher on ourselves! Again, we must not add to a friend's problems as we make our confession. Some people are not equipped to handle a revelation of our sin.

Our real fear, you see, is being rejected once people discover what we are really like. Rejection terrifies us. We protest that we don't care what people think—but we only fool ourselves. We care very much.

God's standards are at this point both merciful and merciless. As the apostle James puts it: "Therefore confess your sins to each other and pray for each other so that you may be healed. The prayer of a righteous man is powerful and effective" (Jas 5:16).

The context is one of prayer for physical healing. But the principle still holds. God's aim is to rid us of the fear of rejection by cleansing us, by making us deeply aware of his own acceptance. We can begin to prepare for God's work as we face that very fear of rejection in confessing our sin to a friend.

But there is something more. Not only does confessing to a friend help heal our fears of rejection and pave the way for receiving God's acceptance. In addition, when we confess to that friend, we begin to be more accountable for our actions.

I have a friend (yes, a friend) who struggled for years with satyriasis, (an abnormal sexual appetite). His problem broke up two marriages. He could make use of several prostitutes in one day. Eventually God moved powerfully into his life, changing him and bringing him through profound repentance. Yet in spite of the change, he would be inclined to slip, especially when feeling down or discouraged. He still needed to learn how to live again.

At that point a male friend felt called by God to be a faithful helper to him. He could sense whenever my friend had slipped and would challenge him to ongoing repentance. In this way my friend learned accountability. It was his final test, his final enabling to enter into the full measure of the change begun in him. Without that friend, to whom he was accountable, the discouragement of a slip might have driven him slowly back to his former state.

My advice, therefore, is to work through these steps along with a friend, either one who has already been through this sort of thing, or one who is going through it at the same time. My own feeling is that it is better that the friend not be a lover or spouse, because complications in the relationship may impede the process.

Step 5 in working toward repentance, then, must be identical with AA's, for it is identical with Scripture: *"God helping me, I will admit to myself, to God, and also to a friend, the exact nature of my sins. Give me a friend, to whom I may be accountable."*

STEP 6: BEING "ENTIRELY READY"

AA's Step 6 is another that assumes you have "hit bottom"—for unless you really have, you can easily deceive yourself on this one. It says: "We were entirely ready to have God remove all these defects of character."

Entirely ready? Sometimes we think we are, but are only fooling ourselves. For the alcoholic attending AA, "entirely ready" includes, among other things, "entirely ready to quit alcohol for the rest of my life." For a true alcoholic, it is ever so hard not to have lingering in an obscure corner of the mind a secret longing that perhaps some day it will be possible to drink safely. A secret relish, too, to manipulate someone else into facilitating the process or to butter up someone for some other wrong reason. Alcoholics are notorious manipulators, and A.A., recognizing manipulative behavior to be a doorway to temptation, challenges it constantly.

We are all the same. We cling to certain unhealthy aspects

of our lives. Some, being inherently sinful, will have to be given up forever. Others, not in themselves sin, but connected to sin in our minds, may have to be given up as well.

Inner dishonesty is our enemy at this point. Psychologists, remember, call it denial. The ancient prophet Jeremiah describes it in more graphic language: "The heart is deceitful above all things and beyond cure. Who can understand it? 'I the LORD search the heart and examine the mind, to reward a man according to his conduct, according to what his deeds deserve'" (Jer 17:9-10).

Deceptive, cunning, untruthful our hearts certainly are. But this fact is no cause for despair. We do not have to wait until our hearts are cleared of all ambivalence. Our scrupulous people have problems at this point. God's first objective in searching our hearts is never judgment, but always healing. Judgment follows our persistent *evasion* of his revelations. His first desire is always to shed light on the dark places of our hearts.

An ancient poet knew this, praying: "Search me, O God, and know my heart; test me and know my anxious thoughts. See if there is any offensive way in me, and lead me in the way everlasting" (Ps 139:23-24).

Therefore Step 6 in working toward repentance is to pray: *Lord, I want to be entirely ready for you to remove every sinful tendency in me. So far as I know, I am ready. But go on testing me, showing me where my motives are phony.*

STEP 7: THE LONGING FOR A CLEAN SLATE

The founders of Alcoholics Anonymous put a great deal of thought into formulating the Twelve Steps. Each step follows closely on the heels of the previous one. Sometimes they seem to be saying almost the same thing, yet they never are. Step 7 is no exception. It seems almost to be a repeat of step 6. But this is not the case.

Step 6 is a preparation for God to do something. Step 7 is the request to God to do what I am now ready to have done. It runs: "We humbly asked him to remove our shortcomings." This step is in essence a request for a clean slate, a blotting out of our record.

Christians see this as entirely biblical. It is exactly what David prayed after he had committed adultery and murder. The consequences of his affair with Bathsheba and his treacherous murder of her husband, Uriah, would bring consequences that dogged David for the rest of his life (see 2 Sm 11-12:18).

Consequences always follow our actions. David knew that, and though he would like to have avoided them, he knew in his heart that he could not. What he wanted more was not an escape from consequences, but forgiveness, a release from the terrible guilt haunting him, a cleansing of the sin itself. This was David's prayer for forgiveness, which God graciously granted: "Have mercy on me, O God, according to your unfailing love; according to your great compassion blot out my transgressions. Wash away all my iniquity and cleanse me from my sin" (Ps 51:1-2).

Whether we realize it or not, freedom from guilt is what constitutes the real beginning of profound change. To know I have been given a fresh start, a clean slate, is spiritually and psychologically necessary if I am to be changed from within. It involves the discovery that I am loved and accepted. Far from making me careless, a deep awareness of forgiveness has precisely the opposite effect. It sets me free to be holy!

The Son of God became a human being and was crucified on our behalf in order to make this forgiveness and freedom from guilt possible. Therefore a modified Step 7 in working toward repentance will be to pray: "*I know you are willing to forgive me, but I ask you to make your forgiveness clear in the deepest parts of my being and not just in my intellect. Show me I am forgiven indeed. Show me the love of Christ as shown on the cross.*"

STEPS 8 AND 9: CLOSING A LOCK

Steps 8 and 9 in working toward repentance follow the eighth and ninth steps of the AA program exactly. If change is to be real, there must first be a willingness to make amends, and then, where it is possible, an acting on that willingness.

The AA step 8 puts it: "We made a list of all persons we had harmed and became willing to make amends to them all." Step 9 follows: "We made direct amends to such people wherever possible."

Such steps represent a closing of the lock on the decisions made in the previous two steps. In and of themselves, these earlier steps do not so much guarantee inner change as open the way to it. They are a test of our genuine desire to change—a test by which we can ourselves measure whether we want to change as much as we *think* we want to.

Only God can bring the change; that is the Holy Spirit's part in bringing about repentance. However, a test of true repentance and of real change is that we are not only willing to make amends, but are unable to tolerate not doing so, so aware are we of the hurt we have caused.

We can see an example of how this works in the story of Zacchaeus found in the New Testament. This despised tax collector once climbed a tree to get a better view of the notorious Jesus. Standing beneath the tree, Jesus called him down. Ever willing to befriend society's rejects, Jesus announced to Zacchaeus that he wanted to visit and have a meal with him.

The shattering impact of the announcement—that a famous figure was willing to associate with him, even to eat at his house, revolutionized the little man's whole life. Zacchaeus said in his excitement, "Look, Lord! Here and now I give half of my possessions to the poor, and if I have cheated anybody out of anything, I will pay back four times the amount" (Lk 19:8). He was not making empty boasts. In the very short time of the interview, Zacchaeus had been changed forever.

The principle of making restitution runs deep in the warp and weft of Judeo-Christian thought. It was early incorporated into the laws of Moses:

> If anyone sins and is unfaithful to the Lord by deceiving his neighbor about something entrusted to him or left in his care or stolen, or if he cheats him, or if he finds lost property and lies about it, or if he swears falsely, or if he commits any such sin that people may do—when he thus sins and becomes guilty, he must return what he has stolen or taken by extortion, or what was entrusted to him, or the lost property he found, or whatever it was he swore falsely about. He must make restitution in full, add a fifth of the value to it and give it all to the owner on the day he presents his guilt offering. (Lv 6:2-5)

More important, it remains today both an essential preparation to repentant change and an evidence of a changed heart.

What then shall the next two steps be in approaching change and repentance? I have only one basic suggestion to add to the AA steps, and that is that we begin our list of persons we have harmed with the persons closest to us—members of our immediate family, and people we meet with every day. These are the ones we usually hurt the most, and certainly they are often (though not always) the most accessible.

Step 8, then, will be: *I make a list of people I have hurt and wronged, beginning with those closest to me. I face before God my responsibility to act.*

Step 9 will follow: *Wherever I can, I will make amends, and do so as soon as possible.*

CHANGE THAT COULD NEVER BE

Change is an inward thing. It has to do with what you are. But an inward change produces changed behavior, a changed lifestyle. In this chapter I have discussed steps, or exercises, that have to do with readiness for that inner change. In the next chapter we can look at the last three steps, which have more to do with ongoing change through an ongoing repentant disposition.

I would like to conclude this chapter, however, with the story of a man who wanted the benefits of change without the pain of it.

My story is set in Florence in the 1490s. The last decade of the century witnessed a strange rivalry between two men: Lorenzo de Medici and Girolamo Savonarola.

Lorenzo was the most colorful of all the Medici family. Banker, prince, military leader, politician, patron of the arts and of philosophers—he played all these roles and more. Lorenzo was also ruthless, power-hungry, and a dilettante who surrounded himself with literary sycophants. This powerful man transformed Florence from a republic to a dictatorship—robbing its citizens of their legal rights, imposing his own benign tyranny, and keeping the citizens happy with a series of fiestas and public spectacles.

But Lorenzo de Medici was debauched, and to maintain his ascendancy, he was frequently both treacherous and cruel. Three cruel acts in particular later haunted him: the sack of a city of Volterra; robbery from the orphanage Monte delle Fanciulle; and the massacre of scores of members of a prominent Florentine family, the Pazzi.

Savonarola, a stark contrast to Lorenzo in most respects, was similar to him in another. Both men were powerful and influential leaders. Savonarola was a Dominican monk whose prophetic zeal and eloquence quickly won large and admiring congregations. Living in a day when popes were corrupt, this Dominican raised his voice fearlessly against what he saw as the sins of Rome.

Savonarola's influence extended far, even to the courtiers who surrounded Lorenzo. Later in his life, he would display astonishing diplomatic abilities that saved Florence from domination by the French. His political power would become so great that eventually his enemies plotted successfully to put him to death by public burning.

That was in the future, however. In Lorenzo's time, Savonarola was widely known and respected. But although leaders among the Dominicans and some of de Medici's courtiers made repeated efforts to get the two men together—both strong leaders, yet so different in their characters—the meeting did not occur until Lorenzo was dying. His death was premature and unexpected, made painful by the stirrings of his conscience over his past cruelties.

While Lorenzo de Medici had no patience with priests and monks, he perceived in Savonarola the integrity and strength of someone who might help him. Messages went back and forth between them. Finally, Savonarola arrived at the deathbed, and Lorenzo was able to unburden his conscience. The historian Burlamacchi gives an account of Savonarola's response:

"Lorenzo," he said, "be not so despairing, for God is merciful to you, if you will do the three things I will tell you."

Then said Lorenzo, "What are these three things?"

The Padre answered, "The first is that you should have a great and living faith that God can and will pardon you."

To which Lorenzo answered, "This is a great thing, and I do believe it."

The Padre added, "It is also necessary that everything wrongfully acquired should be given back by you, in so far as you can do this, and still leave your children as much as will maintain them as private citizens."

These words drove Lorenzo nearly out of himself; but afterwards he said, "This also will I do."

The Padre then went on to the third thing, and said, "Lastly, it is necessary that freedom, and her popular government according to republican usage should be restored to Florence."

At this speech Lorenzo turned his back upon him, nor ever said another word. Upon which the Padre left him and went away without other confession.[5]

Different people reading this account will probably have a different view of what was going on in this interaction. A psychologist might say Savonarola was taking advantage of a dying man's weakness to ram religion down his throat. A politician might say something similar. Was Savonarola merely exploiting Lorenzo's vulnerability to win political freedom for Florence?

Theologians might see the interview in doctrinal terms. Was Savonarola preaching a doctrine of works? Was he saying that Lorenzo had to earn God's forgiveness by making amends for his wrongdoing?

I believe all of these preoccupations miss the Dominican monk's intent. Girolamo Savonarola was suggesting what I have been suggesting throughout this book. The key question and statement is his opening one: "The first [thing you must do] is that you should have a great and living faith that God can and will pardon you."

To which Lorenzo answered, "This is a great thing, and I do believe it."

Lorenzo was quite sincere. He thought he believed, but his "belief" was nothing more than an intellectual acceptance of an idea. The dying man was desperate, but not desperate enough to see himself as he really was. Lorenzo de Medici knew he had done wrong things, and he was troubled by the approach of death. But his deeds were, as it were, outside himself. They were things he had done, as distinct from who and what he was. They affected his reputation, but had little to do with his real person. Or so he thought. He had not seen his own heart. Only such "seeing" could make an inner revolution possible.

It is psychologically impossible to have "a great and living faith" without seeing *from whom* you need to be delivered—namely, yourself. Only then can you appreciate the incredible mercy of the God who is willing to pardon. Lorenzo's heart was unrepentant, and only a repentant heart can know change. He probably looked upon both of the padre's propositions as the price for his willingness to pronounce absolution. Lorenzo was "works oriented." Savonarola was not.

The way you can tell that a person is inwardly changed is that they *want* to make restitution and that they are no longer fearful for their reputation. Lorenzo was not inwardly changed. His responses to Savonarola showed how far he was from even beginning to see the need for a work of God inside his heart.

I believe Savonarola was doing the same thing Jesus was doing when he encountered the wealthy young ruler. Unlike Lorenzo de Medici, the rich ruler prided himself in having kept the law of God rigorously. Responding to Jesus' inquiry, he said, "...all these things have I kept since I was a boy." Lovingly, Jesus responded, "You lack one thing. Sell everything you have and give to the poor, and you will have treasure in heaven. Then come, follow me" (Lk 18:21-22).

Jesus was not teaching that you have to give all your wealth away to get to heaven. He was showing a man who prided himself on outward righteousness what his inner self was really like. Jesus realized with sadness that the man had never seen his heart, and he made a suggestion that would immediately confront him with the real object of his faith—his possessions.

This was precisely what Girolamo Savonarola was aiming

at with Lorenzo de Medici, in his effort to deliver the man from his guilt. And both, unfortunately, "went away sorrowing" and unchanged.

The "steps" I have described in this chapter are designed to help us get in touch with our inner selves. As we take each step we discover our inner reactions to them. Real change has to begin inside us. Outward acts are merely evidence of what is within. It is real change we want. Nothing else is of any use.

NINE

Ongoing Change: The Emergence of the Real Person

The great enemy of the truth is very often not the lie—deliberate, contrived, and dishonest—but the myth, persistent, persuasive, and unrealistic. **John F. Kennedy**

Change in our lifestyle calls for change in our inner selves. The result is the progressive emergence of the person that was meant to be, the realization of our full personhood.

Charles Colson expresses this in terms of the repentance that characterized all real change:

But the repentance God desires of us is not just contrition over particular sins; it is also a daily attitude, a perspective.

Repentance is the process by which we see ourselves, day by day, as we really are: sinful, needy, dependent people. It is the process by which we see God as he is: awesome, majestic and holy.... And [it] so radically alters our perspective that we begin to see the world through God's eyes, not our own. Repentance is the ultimate surrender of the self.[1]

Colson is right. This ultimate, ongoing surrender of the self is the key that allows the real self, the real person to emerge.

REGULAR SELF-ASSESSMENT

I left the last three steps of AA's program to chapters nine and ten precisely because they have to do with ongoing change. Step 10 is: "We continued to take personal inventory and when we were wrong promptly admitted it."

When Ward Gasque began to keep a careful record of *all* he ate, a new struggle quickly emerged; he found he wanted to forget certain items and not write them down. There is nothing like keeping a record for facing our weaknesses, or for keeping the momentum of change going in our lives.

This kind of observation and self-assessment differs enormously from making New Year's resolutions. Rightly conducted, our primary purpose is neither self-oriented nor problem-oriented—but getting to the deepest roots of our difficulties.

In order to maintain the momentum of change in our lives, AA suggests that we continue to take a personal inventory on a regular basis. Some people do this daily, some weekly, others at set times during the year, and yet others annually.

In terms of change and repentance, step 10 can be rephrased as a resolution to God: *I resolve to come before you at certain special times to let you examine my heart and life.*

SELF-ABSORPTION

Self-assessment does have problems, however. We can become either proud or else depressed, depending on our tendencies. In any case, it is helpful to remember that "the spectator sees more of the game." We need someone who knows us better than we know ourselves. Counselors and spiritual directors can help, but King David, you may remember, had an even better thought: he asked God to search his heart, to uncover his offenses, and to lead him to righteousness (see Ps 139:23-24).

More than self-examination, our periodic personal inventory is an invitation to Someone to examine us. The great danger of self-examination is self-absorption. It is so easy to become addicted to scrutinizing one's own navel, either worrying about oneself or being proud of oneself. In either case, I am the center of my attention, and will inevitably become the center of my conversation with others.

The only way to avoid this danger is to be absorbed with someone else. Yet even here we are not quite clear of the danger of self-absorption. I can easily become wrapped up in *my* spouse, *my* kids, *my* siblings, friends, grandchildren etc. Then my supposed absorption in those around me is only one step away from navel-gazing.

I know only one way to avoid the danger: to have one's consciousness turned always to God himself. That is reality. It's a struggle, a tough struggle, but it can be learned. God is a real person, not a psychological state I induce in myself. He is *there*, so to speak, and is always able to interact with us. Turning one's awareness to God is therefore living in reality.

But learning the art of always being turned to God is tough. Oswald Chambers knew it. He said, "In the initial stages it is a continual effort, until it becomes so much the law of life that you abide in Him unconsciously."[2]

Frank Laubach, the great literacy expert, found it a secret that transformed his life.

It is a *will* act. I compel my mind to open straight out toward God. I wait and listen with determined sensitiveness. I fix my attention there, and sometimes it requires a long time in the early morning. I determine not to get out of bed until that mind set upon the Lord is settled.... As for me, I never lived, I was half dead...until I reached the place wholly, with utter honesty, resolved and then re-re-solved that I would find God's will and I would do that will though every fibre in me said no, and I would win the battle *in my thoughts.*[3]

C.S. Lewis was another man who made the same daily effort to live in God's presence. "...The real problem of the Christian life comes... the very moment you wake up each morning. All your wishes and hopes for the day rush at you like wild animals. And the first job each morning consists in shoving them all back; in listening to that other voice, taking that other view, letting that other larger, stronger, quieter life come flowing in. And so on, all day... "[4]

There is nothing far-out about such a life. This should be normal living in the real world. This act of the will is hard to learn only because we have developed other mental habits that need to be unlearned.

PRAYER—THE MEDITATIVE VARIETY

AA's step 11 runs: "We sought through prayer and meditation to improve our conscious contact with God *as we understood him,* praying only for knowledge of his will for us and the power to carry that out." Once again, it is not God-as-you-understand-him that I urge you to seek, but God-as-he-understands-himself. For it is God himself who is seeking you. My understanding is not big enough to measure him. He is real. God understands himself and knows just who he is!

You will have difficulty here if you have not yet found him. Even so, there is everything to be gained by doing what step 11 suggests. But how does one go about prayer and meditation?

I discussed meditation to some extent in chapter seven, but I did not really offer any practical guidelines. How do you go about meditating?

First you need time. You need to take the time, to plan deliberately to take it. Meditation is at once the easiest and yet the most difficult thing in the world. Easy in that it is nothing more than chewing something over in your heart—quietly musing on it. Hard in that when you deliberately try to meditate, you find yourself thinking about any and everything except what you wish to meditate on.

An ancient writer recommends: "I advise that it be once a day at least.... Frequency in contemplation is particularly important to prevent a shyness between God and thy soul."[5] He also states: "Many that make conscience of other duties, easily neglect this. They are troubled if they miss a sermon, a fast, or a prayer... yet were never troubled that they have omitted meditation perhaps all their lifetime... though it be that duty by which all other duties are improved, and by which the soul digests truth for its nourishment and comfort."[6]

So you need to take enough time to waste part of it, enough time to take it easy. It's worth it. You need to be able to relax. When you are "up tight" your thoughts go in circles. Inner stillness is what you need.

Western culture recognizes only one kind of thinking—the analytic, reasoning kind. But there is also the reflective kind, the kind the right hemispheres of our brains were designed for, the musical-poetic-intuitive kind. Curiously, it is this intuitive approach rather than purely analytical reasoning that has led to some of the world's greatest philosophical and scientific discoveries.

Such reflection calls for quiet minds, the kind of quietness and stillness that religious people enter into as they seek God's face. If you've never done it before, you'll find it difficult. You'll be tempted to quit. Don't. Keep at it. The pay off is extremely valuable, even though it takes time. Later, I shall suggest books. One you may find helpful is *The Joy of Listening to God.*[7]

What do you meditate on? Well, if you are still struggling about the reality of God, start with John's Gospel. Or you could try one of the other Gospels. Narrative passages are the easiest to begin with. As you read, ask God to help you picture the scene being described. Listen to the waves on the seashore. Feel the breeze on your face and the sand between your toes. Put yourself in the shoes of one of the characters. Ask yourself what it would be like if Jesus said that (whatever it was!) to you. Get with the story in a way a child would. This approach takes a little time and for some of us a lot of practice (not to say, humbling). But it pays off richly in understanding.

KEEPING A JOURNAL

To start with, keep a journal. Buy yourself a notebook of some kind, and try to spend time every day writing something.

As I suggested in the previous chapter, your struggle with honesty will begin at once. In the first several steps, we were dealing with an initial search for repentance and change. Now we are pursuing on-going change.

Write down the wrong things, the wrong thoughts (hates, jealousies, fears, lusts etc.) which you have entertained over the previous hours. If you have had an argument with someone, deal only with your own failure, not excusing it by the other person's words or attitudes. Whatever you do, do not write anything to justify yourself, or to make yourself appear in a better light.

The idea is not to make yourself look bad, but to paint an honest picture—"warts and all." This process begins to reveal your real problems which underlie the more visible symptoms. My own biggest temptation is to not write down anything that would shock someone else who might read what I have written. So I find myself glossing over certain things I've done or said. God will have none of it. He makes me write in explicit terms, however ugly they make me appear. I hate it while I'm doing it, but I reap enormous benefits afterward.

Remember Ward Gasque again. My impression of Ward is of an exceptionally honest man. Therefore, if Ward found it difficult to remain honest in "journaling," I imagine that most people will.

We live in strange days. Sins abound of which many men and women are proud, alongside others of which everybody is ashamed. Many people can write in their journal that they "went to bed with" some other man or woman in an illicit relationship. Such incidents are not only common, but are taken as a sign of being a normal, "redblooded" man or woman. However, there are other sexual sins of which nobody can be proud.

A friend of mine runs a group for people with sexual perversions of various sorts. Every year the group has new members. The day comes when new members dare to mention "the *m* word"—masturbation. How easy is it to write in one's own journal, "I took my clothes off and masturbated last night?" Or "I was baby-sitting Nancy last night and I molested her?" No one wants to feel like a creep. When you write words like that down in your own journal—you are telling yourself that's what you are.

Yet unless you write down the actual words, you will never learn to be honest with yourself. You know you do or think certain things, but until you write down on paper and re-read what you think and do, you can go on pretending that you are not really the same as other people who do those same things. Somehow you are different—and not quite as bad. Therefore write it all down—neither exaggerating in an orgy of self-pity and self-condemnation, nor excusing or minimizing. Journaling provides a way of taking a good, hard look at yourself in a mirror.

A WRITTEN DIALOGUE

Sometimes (though by no means always) I write my journal as a sort of letter to God. There are days when the letter turns into a dialogue. I make a statement, and God answers. I write his answer down, and then I respond. And so it goes on.

I do this for two reasons. As I mentioned earlier, it is easy for me to write, all the time thinking of an imaginary person looking over my shoulder. If I am not careful, I write *to that audience*, anticipating the person's reactions of admiration or criticism. And it goes without saying that I do not want this imaginary person to think ill of me. Such a way of thinking is the royal road to dishonesty. Very quickly I discover my tendency to edit what I write. When I write to God, I find it easier to be honest.

RELIGIOUS POSTURING AND HONEST PRAYER

Yet even writing to God carries its special temptations to dishonesty. A type of dishonesty characterizes the prayers of all Christians at times. We posture—"get all religious"— when we pray.

I compare it in my mind with going out to tea with my mother when I was small. My mother used to show me off at afternoon tea parties. I was a "good boy." I had been taught how to drink tea politely from china teacups, to respond correctly to invitations to take a sandwich, and so on. I had, of course, been acculturated—reared to behave in a civilized fashion.

But there was still some uncivilized boy left, especially at the tender age of three years. Apparently I was being admired by all the ladies on one occasion and decided to act up. To my mother's acute embarrassment—and her hostess's dismay—I rose to my feet and solemnly and carefully distributed what was left of my tea, letting it dribble across the starched lace table cloth.

My acculturation was at that stage incomplete. But as the years continue, we all learn how to behave on social occasions as well as in our own homes. We do not only behave appropriately, we even think appropriately on most occasions. All the time we think of ourselves as being utterly honest and sincere as we do so. And in a way we are. Yet we are also playing a part, acting a role.

We are playing the part our culture demands that we play. During afternoon tea, it is not usual for a woman to address her friend's husband with, "I would like to go to bed with you." Indeed, *if she has been adequately programmed according to the culture,* she will not even think such thoughts at tea, much less express them. Indeed, she would be shocked and indignant to hear someone else expressing sentiments of that sort. Yet all the while the feeling may be there, the thought hovering in her mind, only to come flooding in later.

In the same way we can play a role when we pray. We put on a sort of spiritual mask. If sinful feelings arise, we frown at them, reminding them that this is not the time or the place for "that sort of thing."

Our prayers are different from the prayers recorded in the Bible. King David often expresses his rage against his enemies, apparently unaware that this is not true spirituality. He slides from, "How precious to me are your thoughts, O God!" to: "Do I not hate those who hate you, O Lord, and abhor those who rise up against you? I have nothing but hatred for them; I count them my enemies" (Ps 139:17,21-22).

This morning I read Psalm 137: "Remember, O Lord, what the Edomites did on the day Jerusalem fell. 'Tear it down,' they cried, 'tear it down to its foundations!' O Daughter of Babylon, doomed to destruction, happy is he who repays you for what you have done to us—*he who seizes your infants and dashes them against the rocks*" (Ps 137:7-9, my italics).

Dashes infants against the rocks? This prayer certainly does not express "spiritual" sentiments. Is it ever right to fling a helpless child against rocks, battering it to death? Surely this is an appalling prayer! We do not even allow ourselves to think that kind of thought.

Unlike the psalmist, we are basically dishonest. You may insist, "But in God's presence we should show reverence. God is holy."

This may be so. But if our hearts are full of lust and rage, while we pretend reverence, are we not piling sin on sin, deception on deception? If there is any place where we must be ourselves, surely it is in God's presence. I do not deny the importance of reverence, but it must be true reverence—not an actor's attempt to play a reverent character, while hate and rage make mayhem in his heart.

Whenever I have given way to my true feelings, even wrongfully and sinfully, God has revealed himself to me as never before. Only four times in my life have I seen a vision of God himself. On one occasion I flung myself on my study carpet, enraged with God for what I thought was his heartless treatment of my second son. "What kind of a Father do you call yourself?" I cried, beating the floor with my fists. All of a sudden the floor appeared to open up, and I found myself looking down on a beach as huge green breakers crashed onto the yellow sand.

Instantly I knew that the sea was God. I was in his immediate presence and terrified. Worse, the crashing waves were his compassion. I had expected his anger and had sinfully defied it. In response God had shown me the greatness of his concern. I trembled violently and wept bitterly and long, not angry with him any more, but profoundly repentant over the hardness and shallowness of my own heart.

We need to plunge into the depths of our own hearts when we pray. Even when we find ourselves in uncharted regions with sordid secrets we have never seen before—we will find God was already there to welcome us in love. His love takes him deeper than the vilest part of our natures. That is why we must cultivate reality in praying.

And in journaling. They are both part of the same process. As we wait on God, we will begin to discover what he is like. And with that discovery, we will begin to change more and more.

LEARNING TO LISTEN

"But what about God's replies," you may ask. "Are those imaginary, or real?"

Good question! They can be either, depending on whether you have learned to distinguish his voice. "But how can you be so sure?" you ask. "How do you know you're not just imagining the replies? Surely you don't actually hear a voice?"

No, as a matter of fact I have never heard a voice. Yet I am getting to the point where I know the precise words that I must write in my journal. God does not just make statements, but exact statements. He also asks questions—very penetrating ones. For me, learning to hear God's voice has been a lengthy learning experience. But the nature of the questions has astonished me most. I never knew God thought about me the way he does.

A book entitled *Dialogue With God* expresses my own experience. The author states: "In my journal, I find that God always talks to me about my attitudes. He speaks of my anger, my scorn, my judgement. He tells me to honor, to love, to receive. He's much more concerned about the attitudes that cause my sins than about the sins themselves, and He wants very much to heal me of those attitudes. He hates sin, but He always works to root out its causes, not just to end our wrong actions."[8]

That's it exactly. God wants to root out the causes of the undesirable behavior. If the cause of it can be removed, then the behavior can be permanently changed. But I have to be able to hear his voice. Sometimes there are days, even weeks, when I hear nothing. Then it starts again.

I hear more clearly now than ever before. The Bible describes a God who is always speaking to human beings. He is essentially a communicating God, but one whose voice we have to learn to hear.

Jesus talks about this sort of thing, comparing us to sheep, and himself to a shepherd. "The man who enters by the gate is the shepherd of his sheep... and the sheep listen to his voice. He calls his own sheep by name and leads them out. When he has brought out all his own, he goes on ahead of them, and his sheep follow him *because they know his voice.* But they will never follow a stranger; in fact, they will run away from him *because they do not recognize a stranger's voice*" (Jn 10:2-5, italics mine).

Jesus is telling us a number of things. You will notice first that he is talking about sheep, not lambs. Sheep hear and pay attention to a shepherd's voice in the Middle East. Lambs do not. Lambs respond to the call of their mothers. Responding to the shepherd's voice is an acquired skill, demanding patience on the part of the shepherd as he trains the growing sheep. In the same way we need to learn to distinguish between the voice of the shepherd, our own thoughts, and the suggestions of evil.

Years ago when I first started to keep a journal, I would record as accurately as I could what I thought God was saying, leaving space to comment later as to whether subsequent events proved me right or wrong. Often I was astonishingly right, at other times abysmally wrong. However I learned. I would pray and ponder over the times when I had been mistaken, gradually becoming more aware of what "God's voice" really sounded like.

A PERSONAL RELATIONSHIP

"He calls his own sheep by name."

An Eastern shepherd names each sheep, learns their idiosyncrasies, thinks of them almost as his children. Eastern shepherds differ from Australian or New Zealand sheep farmers, who have a more impersonal view of the sheep, thinking rather of economics, of the type, the fibre length and thickness of wool, and so on.

Like the Eastern shepherd, God has a name for you. He may not—certainly for many years—reveal that name. The important point to grasp is that God longs for an intimate and personal relationship with you. He never thinks of your commercial value—only of your person, and of his longing that you know him better.

Earlier I mentioned how hard this was for me to grasp. One day I was reflecting on the expression *Abba*, the name by which both Jesus and St. Paul describe God the Father, a name which in Aramaic means "daddy." I cried out, "I just can't call YOU daddy!" As quick as a flash the answer came back, "But I *am* your daddy!"

In view of the intimacy which God longs to share with us, it makes no sense that he should not communicate with us directly, nor that he would not teach us to hear and to respond.

THE DANGERS

Earlier we discussed evil and evil beings. Many Christians become almost paranoid at the thought of them. Some would prefer to hear nothing, lest they hear "from the other side" and get fooled and misled.

This is the height of folly. God is greater than any enemy. He cares too much to let us be led astray when we try to hear his own voice. You may hear nothing at times, but he will not allow you to be misled—unless you want to be.

Listen again to Christ's own statement on the matter: "His sheep follow him *because they know his voice*. But they will never follow a stranger; in fact, they will run away from him *because they do not recognize a stranger's voice*" (Jn 10:4-5).

It is true that at the height of a psychotic experience even a Christian may lose the capacity temporarily to distinguish God's voice from others. But the loss is only temporary. As the person recovers, so does the ability to distinguish the voice of the true shepherd. Moreover, even at the height of the psychosis, though the person may suffer pain, they will never be drawn away from the Lord's care and ownership.

If you can find someone who knows more about this meditative kind of prayer than you do, then compare notes from time to time. Get advice from more experienced people. Beware of being proud when you think you have heard from God. Pride and self-congratulation are deadly. Be slow to talk about it. All you have learned is to be a little more childlike, or sheep-like!

THE PROOF OF THE PUDDING

If you are going about it the right way, four more things will be happening in addition to becoming less self-absorbed: you will experience mingled pain and joy; you will come to a deepening appreciation of Christ's death and resurrection; you will grow more intimate with God; and finally, you will become closer to people all around you, more concerned about them, more friendly toward them. If meditative prayer isolates you from others over the long run, or if you start having fantastic visions without the pain of discovering more of your own sin and weakness—then watch out! You are probably on the wrong track.

Firstly, you will experience mingled joy and pain. The discovery of sin, weaknesses, despicable aspects of your character, painful memories from the past—all of these are ongoing. All will involve repentance, sometimes with weeping. But with the pain comes a fresh marvelling at God's loving concern for you.

From these discoveries come ongoing, permanent change in your character. In my case it is the love that makes me weep, not the pain of seeing my failures. Seeing God's kindness moves me profoundly. As St. Paul puts it as he comments on our tendency to criticize others while ignoring our own faults: "Or do you show contempt for the riches of his kindness, tolerance and patience, not realizing that God's kindness leads you toward repentance?" (Rom 2:4). The mingling of pain and joy are what Paul refers to as godly sorrow. Repentance and change come that way: "Godly sorrow brings repentance that leads to salvation and leaves no regret, but worldly sorrow brings death" (2 Cor 7:10).

This progressive character change is what theologians call sanctification—at least the way sanctification gets worked out in practice. We progressively enter into full personhood, the personhood that most resembles the completeness of Jesus Christ, even while we retain our personal distinctiveness.

You are not responsible for producing holiness within yourself. God assumes that responsibility. Like a physician, he tells you what to do, what remedy to apply next. In this way your attention can remain centered in God, and thus avoid being self-absorbed.

Secondly, you will have a deepening awareness of the significance of the death and resurrection of Jesus Christ. Some of this

will come from meditating upon accounts of his death and
the resurrection in the Bible. The knowledge of what they
mean theologically and historically is not enough. The puritan Richard Baxter puts it very poetically, using "consideration" as another term for meditation: "*Consideration*, as it
were, opens the door between the head and the heart."⁹

Thirdly, you will become more intimate with God. You will get
to know him, and to enjoy a closer and more loving relationship. This may take time. It is difficult to conceive of a
Creator God in this way, let alone to experience it. To do so
involves a good deal of unlearning for some of us. You may
experience fear, even dread, in route to intimacy. For me it
has involved trembling with dread.

Finally, you will become closer to people all around you. Any
proximity to God that comes at the expense of distance from
other people is a delusion. Progress consists of becoming
more outward-oriented, less self-centered, simultaneously
God-centered and other-centered. When Jesus was asked
what was the one great commandment, he refused to stop at
one and gave two: "Love the Lord your God with all your
heart and with all your soul and with all your mind. This is
the first and greatest commandment. And the second is like
it: Love your neighbor as yourself" (Mt 22:37-39).

Love of God goes with love of one's neighbor. Clearly,
Jesus thinks of these as inseparably linked. The closer a person is to one, the closer they will be to the other. The more
easily I can talk with God, the more readily will I communicate with my neighbor. I deceive myself if I feel my spirituality makes it harder to communicate with people around me.
True spirituality makes me more ordinary, more easy to
know.

"When you go deep into God in prayer, you do not leave
this world.... Do not believe those who tell you that the service of God stops you from being dedicated, body and soul,
to your brothers. This talk belongs to the 'religious parrotry'
of our epoch."¹⁰

A BIRTHDAY PARTY FOR HOOKERS

If anyone ever demonstrated this other-centeredness, Jesus Christ did. All the Gospel accounts tell us that sinners flocked around him. His love for God brought him into contact with all manner of men and women, none of whom seemed to find him an embarrassment. Nor did Jesus consider them an embarrassment to him. It was the religious hierarchy who had difficulty with Jesus. And frequently, his association with disreputable types was a particular source of criticism by religious groups.

Churches and religious people today do not make friends easily with people who are looked down on in society—jail birds, prostitutes, drug addicts, drunks, thieves. This suggests that they may not be so near to God as they suppose. "Sinners" do not find churches attractive, so that sinners and would-be saints often keep to their respective ghettos.

However, there are refreshing exceptions to the rule. Tony Campolo, professor of sociology at Eastern College, tells the story of his visit to Honolulu for a Christian Conference. On his first night there, he awoke sometime after three (a six hour time difference had confused his sleep pattern) and left the hotel in search of a place to get something to eat. Eventually he found a tiny coffee shop, with one man behind the bar who served him coffee and a doughnut.

Tony was the only customer until, quite suddenly, the coffee shop was filled with girls. Some sat at small tables, others at the counter near Tony. From their conversation he learned an astonishing amount about Honolulu's night life, for the girls were discussing their night's work and their male clients. These girls were prostitutes. He tells the story:

> I overheard the woman sitting beside me say, "Tomorrow's my birthday. I'm going to be thirty-nine."
>
> Her "friend" responded in a nasty tone, "So what do you want from me? A birthday party? What do you want?

Ya want me to get you a cake and sing 'Happy Birthday'?"

"Come on!" said the woman sitting next to me. "Why do you have to be so mean? I was just telling you, that's all. Why do you have to put me down? I was just telling you it was my birthday. I don't want anything from you. I mean, why should you give me a birthday party? I've never had a birthday party in my whole life. Why should I have one now?

When I heard that, I made a decision. I sat and waited until the women had left. Then I called over the fat guy behind the counter and I asked him, "Do they come in here every night?"

"Yeah!" he answered.

"The one right next to me, does she come here every night?"

"Yeah!" he said. "That's Agnes. Yeah, she comes in here every night. Why d'ya wanta know?"

"Because I heard her say that tomorrow is her birthday," I told him. "What do you say you and I do something about that? What do you think about us throwing a birthday party for her—right here—tomorrow night?"

A cute smile slowly crossed his chubby cheeks and he answered with measured delight, "That's great!... "Look, I told them, "if it's O.K. with you, I'll get back here tomorrow morning about 2:30 and decorate the place. I'll even get a birthday cake!"

"No way," said Harry (that was his name). "The birthday cake's my thing. I'll make the cake."

At 2:30 the next morning, I was back at the diner. I had picked up some crepe-paper decorations at the store and had made a sign out of big pieces of cardboard that read, "Happy Birthday, Agnes!" I decorated the diner from one end to the other. I had that diner looking good.

The woman who did the cooking must have gotten the word out on the street, because by 3:15 every prostitute in

Honolulu was in the place. It was wall-to-wall prostitutes... and me!

At 3:30 on the dot, the door of the diner swung open and in came Agnes and her friend. I had everybody ready (after all, I was kind of the M.C. of the affair) and when they came in we all screamed, "Happy birthday!"

Never have I seen a person so flabbergasted... so stunned... so shaken. Her mouth fell open. Her legs seemed to buckle a bit. Her friend grabbed her arm to steady her. As she was led to sit on one of the stools along the counter we all sang "Happy Birthday" to her. As we came to the end of our singing with "happy birthday dear Agnes, happy birthday to you," her eyes moistened. Then, when the birthday cake with all the candles on it was carried out, she lost it and just openly cried.

Harry gruffly mumbled, "Blow out the candles, Agnes! Come on! Blow out the candles! If you don't blow out the candles, I'm gonna hafta blow out the candles." And, after an endless few seconds, he did. Then he handed her a knife and told her, "Cut the cake, Agnes. Yo, Agnes, we all want some cake."

Agnes looked down at the cake. Then without taking her eyes off it, she slowly and softly said, "Look, Harry, is it all right with you if I... I mean is it O.K. if I kind of... want I want to ask you is... is it O.K. if keep the cake a little while? I mean is it all right if we don't eat it right away?"

Harry shrugged and answered, "Sure! It's O.K. If you want to keep the cake, keep the cake. Take it home if you want to."

"Can I?" she asked. Then, looking at me she said, "I live just down the street a couple of doors.,, I want to take the cake home, O.K.? I'll be right back. Honest!"

She got off the stool, picked up the cake, and, carrying it like it was the Holy Grail, walked slowly toward the door.

As we all just stood there motionless, she left.

When the door closed there was a stunned silence in the place. Not knowing what else to do, I broke the silence by saying, "What do you say we pray?"

Looking back on it now it seems more than strange for a sociologist to be leading a prayer meeting with a bunch of prostitutes in a diner in Honolulu at 3:30 in the morning. But then it just felt like the right thing to do. I prayed for Agnes. I prayed for her salvation. I prayed that her life would be changed and that God would be good to her.

When I finished, Harry leaned over the counter and with a trace of hostility in his voice, he said "Hay! You never told me you were a preacher. What kind of church do you belong to?"

In one of those moments when just the right words came, I answered, "I belong to a church that throws birthday partied for whores at 3:30 in the morning."

Harry waited a moment and then almost sneered as he answered, "No you don't. There's no church like that. If there was, I'd join it. I'd join a church like that!"[11]

Tony Campolo had displayed the behavior of a truly repentant person in whom on-going change was taking place. He lacked the stuffy pseudo-Christian religious posturing that is mistaken by so many people for spirituality. He was being real.

The world is hungry, aching with longing for people like that.

TEN

Persuasion—Or Manipulation?

Zounds! I was never so bethumped with words
Since I first called my brother's father, dad.
Shakespeare (King John)

A word aptly spoken is like apples of gold in settings of sil-
ver. **Prv 25:11**

I n the previous two chapters we looked at eleven of AA's twelve steps. As we did so, we began to see that they were related to the two concepts that have come to occupy our attention—change and repentance.

Only the last of the twelve steps remains to be examined. At this point, the alcoholic who has benefited from practicing the AA principles resolves to continue this new lifestyle and to "carry the message" to fellow strugglers. The twelfth step reads, "Having had a spiritual awakening as the result of these steps, we tried to carry this message to alcoholics, and to practice these principles in all our affairs."

No one objects to people "doing their thing." If alcoholics wish to practice the twelve steps all their lives, well and good. But is it everyone's thing? Should people who benefit from certain principles feel obligated to pass them on to others?

Alcoholics Anonymous "carries the message" to alcoholics in a number of ways. They try to avoid ego trips by keeping public functionaries as low-key as possible. While they use public speakers, the most important work is one-on-one sharing with fellow strugglers. Their zeal and enthusiasm in sharing their personal experience can almost seem evangelistic. While their concern for those still suffering is real, recovering alcoholics have a somewhat selfish motivation. They have become convinced that if they don't reach out to help others, they will eventually sink back into their own unhealthy habits. Carrying this message to others helps to insure their continuing sobriety and recovery from the disease of alcoholism.

If in this book we have discovered principles that can bring radical and permanent change in our lives, ought we to pass on those principles? Sharing can mean anything from not minding our own business, to making a thorough nuisance of ourselves. Is "twelfth step work" of interest to those of us who are not alcoholics, but have discovered divine power changing us? What about the warnings I gave earlier concerning manipulative techniques? What role does persuasion play in change?

Helping others is a human duty. Yet it has dangers. We must understand what those dangers are, and how we may help without hurting others. This final chapter will discuss the psychology, the morality, and the theology of sharing good news.

EMOTION AND EMOTIONALISM

We became aware in the first chapter that there are people who are extremely good at manipulating other people's emotions. Some people do it just for kicks. They may enjoy a feeling of power when a crowd seems to be hanging on their every word. They can be tempted to play on others' feelings as if playing a musical instrument or conducting an orchestra. Power gives some people a high, a boost for their ego.

But before long the lust for power grows. Manipulating people from a platform is not enough. They may want political power, religious power—more power of any kind over other people. Slowly a state of mind develops in which people are only important as a means of gaining their own ends. Others are viewed only as useful or useless tools. People in power search for a population base, crowds who will vote for them, riot for them, attack their enemies.

It is easy to see why persuasion has always been a part of human society. But persuasion has two sides to it. Honest persuasion is good and necessary. Artificial manipulation of emotion is evil.

Persuasion impacts every aspect of life. Among our earliest memories are those of being persuaded. "Eat it up, now. You'll never be a big boy if you don't eat your cereal!" "Crusts make your hair curl. I always ate my crusts!" "What do you mean, you can't? Of course you can. You did it yesterday." Some of us are suckers and let ourselves be persuaded too easily. Others of us are paranoid, missing great opportunities that life presents because our fears and suspicions get in the way.

The free enterprise system would not work without persuasion, for the key person in our free enterprise system is the salesperson. The most successful ones are those who excel at persuading people to buy what they sell. The greatest ally of the sales person is a creative copy writer. Words are powerful tools, powerful for good and for evil. An expert copy writer can make you see the beauty and wisdom of murdering your own mom.

In Western history persuasion began with the Greeks and their passion for elocution, or persuasion from a public platform. The power of words affected law, politics, religion, and commerce. In all these areas persuasion is as powerful for evil as for good. For every wise and righteous statesman, there is a Rasputin; for every honest politician, a clever pro-propagandist. For every godly religious leader, there is a Jim Jones; for every just judge, a corrupt one; and for every business executive who is seen as a public benefactor and philanthropist, a fly-by-night shyster and scam-artist.

We are dealing, however, with repentance and changed characters. We want to be sure that persuasion applied in an effort to induce repentance is honest persuasion—not a shameless manipulation of human emotion. An honest persuader tells the truth. An honest persuader does not play mind games with the cunning use of words.

BRAIN WASHING

Brain washing is easy if you know how. One way to do it—if you are enough of a scoundrel to try—is to fool around with what are called people's *percepts*. Manipulating perceptual input is a way of getting people anxious and confused. Once they are anxious and confused, you make use of exhaustion—keep your victims going for hours on end. Most important of all, you should try to make them feel guilty.

Let me express this in technical language. You change the volume of *perceptual input*, introduce *perceptual incongruity*, induce a sense of false guilt, and make use of exhaustion and sleeplessness. In this way you can become an arch manipulator. Basically you treat people as though they were laboratory animals or machines. You program them.

Percept is a psychological term. When light through the window strikes your eye, you do not "see a tree" through the window—you form a percept. Many complicated processes take place in your brain in a flash. Your eye is like a camera whose lens projects an upside down image of a tree on your retina. Without your conscious effort or awareness, your brain rapidly organizes colors and shapes your eye has presented to it, turns the image the right way up, checks it against other shapes and colors, and comes up with the word "tree." You say, "I see a pine tree." The pine tree is the *percept* your brain has organized.

We can further classify it as a *congruous* percept. The tree is in the proper place—on the neighbor's lawn. If, on the other hand the tree were upside down—balanced precariously on its tip and displaying its roots to the sky—you would feel bewildered. The words that your brain would come up with in that case might be, "What on earth... ?"

Your upside down tree would be an *incongruous* percept, a *perceptual incongruity, something that did not match the rest of your experience.* This incongruity would cause you to doubt your senses. You might even feel scared.

Some new ideas, even if true, are *incongruous percepts.* The word incongruous does not mean bad. Rather it means that the new idea clashes with other ideas in your mind. Remember the maps of reality we talked about earlier? To discover your map is wrong is to be presented with an incongruous percept. You experience anxiety and dismay in some degree. Anxiety is part of finding the truth, a necessary part of exploring reality. It is therefore an inevitable part of true repentance, and of real character change.

The washer of brains (and the conscience-less copy writer) is not primarily concerned with truth, however, but with persuasion. And when persuasion becomes too important to us, we treat our fellow humans as machines or morons.

Political propaganda deals with masses in this way—by reducing a nation to an anonymous mass of bodies, welded into a political machine. One minister of state in a foreign country told a friend of mine, "I want a pre-tuned television set in every village. That way I don't need to worry about literacy. I can control the whole country."

PERCEPTUAL OVERLOAD

There is more to percepts than incongruity. When we talk about *perceptual input,* we are talking about something more than the stimuli that bombard you. We are including all the work your brain and central nervous system do to organize and make sense of the incoming data.

Perceptual overload makes us anxious. We get used to a level of input that is peculiar to each of us. Some of us like soft background music. We hardly notice it. If we turn up the volume a little to hear something we like, we become mildly anxious. Because our anxiety is only mild, we refer to it as pleasure—a sort of heightening of our awareness.

We all have a preferred level of perceptual input. The percepts are organized in our brains from our sensory data—what we see, hear, touch, taste, and smell. We grow unpleasantly anxious, restless, even fearful when the input is greatly increased or greatly reduced. Loud rock music usually drives older people crazy. Our lack of appreciation has a lot to do with the greatly increased perceptual input. Children like to be tickled—a little. But tickling can be an agony when taken too far.

Just as too much perceptual input makes you anxious, too little has the same result. Absolute silence tends to unnerve people who live in the center of a large city. In one experiment volunteers were suspended in warm water, blindfolded, naked, wearing earplugs and breathing through an air tube. The experimenters were trying to cut down perceptual input. The subjects became disoriented, anxious, and confused. They experienced *perceptual underload*.

On the other hand, picture yourself driving your car through downtown traffic with a carload of noisy, quarrelling children. The radio is too loud and your bladder is frantically signalling "full, full, FULL!" Signals are thus coming from traffic patterns, stop lights, other drivers, the radio, your kids, and your bladder. All these signals are demanding attention.

Technically speaking, you are experiencing perceptual overload, a higher level of perceptual input than is normally comfortable for you. Your feelings will verge on desperation and you may begin to behave accordingly.

HOW TO AVOID MANIPULATION

We want to understand which human "buttons" to avoid pressing if we are to be true persuaders, rather than power-hungry brain washers. So far I may have given you the impression that technical knowledge is the key to the matter. It isn't. What matters are the motives of our hearts when engaged in persuasion.

Whenever our motive in persuading people is selfish—to make money, to gain adherents, to boost our own egos, or to increase our political or professional status—we are in danger of becoming manipulators rather than persuaders. Many people stumble onto brain washing principles without having any background knowledge. In their effort to gain their own ends, they find certain ploys work, and they go on using them.

Sad to say, all sectors of human society are subject to too much manipulation and too little honest persuasion. Persuasion must address itself to a person's understanding. A manipulator subtly directs words at someone's emotions.

The object in both cases is a decision. But the decision must be made freely by the person making the decision. A good persuader is a person who presents truth to a person's mind, and shows the relevance of that truth to the person's conscience.

MAKING DECISIONS

Four components go into making a decision: mind; conscience (or super-ego); emotions; and will (or volition).

The *mind* is what ancient writers called *understanding*. It is important to understand what you are getting into before you make a decision. When you buy a stereo system, for example, you need to know things like how it works, how simple it is to operate, whether it suits your requirements, whether there is a guarantee, how much it costs, and so on. So you inquire, you think, you try to understand.

Conscience is triggered if some kind of "ought" is involved. Perhaps you had promised the money to someone else. Maybe you should be buying medication for yourself, or using that money to pay off a long-standing debt. Your conscience might be arguing against the purchase.

Emotions were discussed in chapter seven. If your conscience is acting up, you may grow anxious and restless. You may even lose sleep over the purchase. On the other hand, you may take home some glossy hand-outs from the store, with beautiful pictures of the stereo and enticing descriptions of its performance. As you read them you grow more and more excited about owning it. Conscience is slowly being drowned out by pleasing emotions.

Finally there is *will*, or *volition*. Either I make a decision to buy this particular stereo system or to refrain from buying it, at least for now. The outcome of my decision-making process will depend on the interplay between understanding, conscience, emotion, and will.

Let me go through the process again. A persuasive person—perhaps a salesman, a public speaker, a writer, or a friend presents me with information. I process the information through my mind, conscience, emotions, and volition before I make a decision.

I begin by carefully thinking through the information. The main question in my mind must be: Is this true? Does this information represent a doorway to reality?

The next question will be: Is there something I ought to do about it? By this time my emotions may be stirred. Part of me may want to ignore the information, to deny any truth in it. Another part of me may long for it to be true, whether it is true or not. I may glimpse either a doorway to reality, or a slip-way into a world of delusions. For mind is not an independent entity. I do not operate in pure logic. No man or woman does. Mr. Spock does not exist. Conflicting emotions, a disturbed conscience, and understanding all wrestle among themselves.

The job of the manipulator at this point is to side with whichever of my conflicted emotions goes along with his or her agenda. Manipulators will plug emotion, conscience, or reason to suit their purposes—whether or not the resulting decision is to your benefit or in the direction of reality.

Therefore put yourself into the shoes of the person being persuaded. You wouldn't want to be fooled yourself—so don't try to "pull a fast one" over on anyone else. If you have a gift of speaking clearly and logically, be grateful. But never forget that you have in that gift a weapon that can destroy lives as well as heal and help them. Don't be a con-artist.

THE RELIGIOUS CON-ARTIST

Years ago I used to serve as a counselor for evangelistic campaigns. Gradually I began to see that some evangelists manipulated their congregations. I cannot say that they always realized what they were doing. Somehow in their desire to see people "come to the front" for counseling, they had intuitively learned how to press the right buttons in their listeners, how to gain control over their audience.

Sometimes an evangelist would tell moving stories, not so much to illustrate a point as to create an emotion. Then he would exploit the solemn mood to provoke awe, then fear and anxiety. Then he would tell a joke, so that people would laugh. But you could feel a sense of relief: the joke had released some of the tension. After that there would be another solemn story. Then another joke.

Before long some of the folks were having a good time. "He's a marvelous speaker!" they would whisper. Other people, who were new to the game, would look either a little dazed or a little distressed. They had lost their bearings. The speaker had reproduced in them the state of mind due to over-stimulation, with incongruous percepts and perceptual overload.

The speaker would sense that the crowd was "under conviction." But they were not truly under conviction of their sinfulness. Their condition was psychological—not the distress brought about by that appalling clarity of perception that the Spirit of God alone can produce. It was poles removed from what Chuck Colson experienced, or the Welsh Christians I described in chapter one.

However, some in the audience would undergo a psychological transformation that could be mistaken for Christian conversion. Like the Chinese students, they would experience peace and joy—temporarily. But theirs would not be a true transformation, but only a pseudo change. In most cases (as I soon found out), they would become hostile and run a mile rather than meet anyone who represented the organizers of the meeting. They had been the victims of preaching, which consciously or unconsciously depended on manipulation rather than on the Spirit of God.

In contrast, I was recently present at a crowded conference where a preacher taught from the Bible without any manipulation. Most people sat in a main auditorium, while others watched the speaker on television in two large side rooms. I was in one of the side rooms.

The speaker was in earnest. But his earnestness arose from his concern about the truth of what he was saying. He was sharing his heart without any attempt to play on people's feelings. It is one thing to be moved yourself, and quite another to use your emotions to manipulate others. Before long people in my room began to leave their seats and kneel at the front. The speaker had not gotten even half way into his address, and had made no such suggestion.

Curious, I went to the main auditorium to see what was taking place there. Sure enough, people were doing the same thing. For a time the speaker ignored what was happening. Soon people were moving into the aisles. Some were weeping, others praying. They seemed unaware of the people around them.

The preacher stopped and turned to consult two other men on the platform. Then, hesitantly, he began to preach for a little longer. But soon the whole body of people in the room were "doing their own thing." Instead of preaching, the speaker began to pray aloud for the people before him.

What I saw on that occasion was a total contrast from what I had observed in my youth (and many times since). The speaker himself seemed at a loss to account for what was happening, and had certainly not produced it. This emotional outpouring was a work of the Holy Spirit, not a product of human psychology.

THE PERSUADER

What, then, *is* the persuader's true role?

St. Paul was a Jewish Roman citizen who had strong ideas on the art of persuasion. He had been trained in the best rabbinical tradition under a superb professor named Gamaliel. He also seems to have had some training in elocution. As a Jew, Paul viewed Jesus as the Messiah who was to come. But he faced opposition in talking about his convictions from Jew and Gentile alike. Paul was actually a poor public speaker. Yet his writings and life are more carefully studied than those of any other Christian to this day.

What does Paul say about his own mission to persuade? In the face of bitter persecution and rejection, he writes, "...we do not lose heart. Rather, we have renounced secret and shameful ways; we do not use deception, nor do we dis-

tort the word of God. On the contrary, by setting forth the
truth plainly we commend ourselves to every man's conscience in the sight of God" (2 Cor 4:1-2).

It is clear from his other letters that Paul did not wish to
fool around with people's emotions. His mention of "secret
and shameful ways" and the use of deception probably referred to the commonly used elocution techniques of his day.
Paul was determined to present what he saw to be reality
without any verbal tricks. His only desire was to present the
material as clearly as possible, knowing that the truth itself
would awaken someone's conscience.

But Paul was aware of something else. There were "hidden persuaders" of a nonhuman variety, and Paul knew it.
He saw that behind evil and sin were the Dark Powers we
discussed earlier in chapter four. He comments, "If our
gospel is veiled, it is veiled to those who are perishing. The
god of this age has blinded the minds of unbelievers, so that
they cannot see the light... of the glory of Christ... " (2 Cor
4:3-4).

Knowing what he did, this evangelist saw the folly of rely-
ing on manipulation. Manipulation is effective for evil, never
for good. It cannot do God's work. It can gain converts—but
what sort of converts? Ours, not God's. St. Paul knew that
God himself had to do the work no human being has the
wisdom or the integrity to do. Only by the grace of God can
a troubled person find truth, find reality, find Christ, find
God himself.

Paul's job was to present truth. Truth itself stirs conscience. God's job is to handle the conflict that arises with
emotions, the confusion of will, the bewilderment—by gen-
tly revealing the truth to the inward heart.

If we are persuaders let us confine ourselves to presenting
truth clearly. Let us leave the rest to God.

Most people would agree with me that some Christian
leaders are no different from unprincipled advertising copy-
writers and sales persons. Like anyone else who gains their

livelihood by selling a product, they "sell" Christianity by manipulation, elocution, and trickery. They use their skill with words to gain control over an audience.

How then should the preacher preach? Ought he ever to awaken emotion? What spells the difference between honest preaching and "secret and shameful ways?" How can public speakers make what they have to say interesting, without conning people? How can they awaken men and women to the seriousness of the topic without inducing mass hysteria? And how does genuine feeling, even strong emotion in a crowd of people differ from mass hysteria and panic?

The key to all these questions commonly lies in the attitude of the speaker. The ideal preacher knows three things. First he (I shall say *he*, since the male is commoner, and I detest she-or-he-isms) must know that the business of getting people in touch with reality is God's business. Being awakened to reality arouses strong emotions in people.

Second, the preacher must realize that God is present and delights to awaken people. Thirdly, the preacher himself must be in touch with reality, having spent enough time in the presence of God to have been awakened himself. In this way, he will realize the solemnity of his task.

If he knows his business, the preacher will also be in touch with the Holy Spirit as he delivers the message God has given him. Though solemnly aware of God's intent, he will not try to induce an emotional state in people, but will focus on presenting truth as simply and clearly as possible. What was it Paul said as he discussed minds blinded by evil powers: "… by setting forth the truth plainly we commend ourselves to every man's conscience in the sight of God."

"Setting forth truth" means making something clear, explaining reality plainly. The honest preacher uses comprehensible language and easily grasped biblical ideas and truths. The point of any illustrations or tells stories should be obvious. "Tear jerkers" and pointless humor are out.

However, if he does his job well, reality itself will touch

the consciences of his listeners. The preacher's job is never to "lay guilt trips" on his listeners. Inducing guilt is God's job. God awakens conscience to reality. The preacher presents truth (or reality) "in the sight of God."

But as we have already seen, an awakened conscience involves awakened emotions. It is at this point that we must understand the difference between crowd hysteria and the emotions that arise in people who happen to be crowded into the same place. The two are poles apart. Crowd hysteria is a panic induced by a mass sense of unreal terror, a momentary psychosis, a move away from reality.

Previously I described a panic that seized the members of a New England congregation two and a half centuries ago. The panic caused men and women to cling to the pillars of the church building, fearing they might be swept away into hell at any moment. No eloquence was at the root of their terror. Rather the Spirit of God was moving powerfully, awakening the congregation to reality.

The congregation did not crowd the doorways in a panic to escape, as do people trapped in a burning building. They knew flight was useless. They cried out to God for pardon as they saw the gravity of their condition. The panic was fear in the face of terrible reality, reality to which they had been awakened for the first time in their lives.

The weeping of the congregation in the Welsh village is an excellent example of the same dynamic. On that occasion no preacher was even preaching. Instead, the preacher stood mute in the face of the congregation's criticism.

Let me repeat the quotation from the diary of a man who was present: "One of the elders got up and said it was a very difficult thing for a man to say 'Amen' under a ministry he felt condemning him; and as he said these things he sat down as if fainting away. At this moment, there was something (I cannot say what it was, but that it was *something* that neither I nor any one else had ever felt before) went through the whole congregation, until every one put down his head and wept!"[1]

The "something that neither I nor any one else had ever felt before" was the Divine Presence. It is God who awakens our consciences to life and our persons to reality. The Welsh Calvinists were not overwhelmed by mass hysteria, but by those emotions that are a prelude to emotional health, to lives lived in the light of reality. A world of difference separates the two.

THE ROLE OF A WITNESS

Few of us are public speakers, but all of us should bear witness to the truth whenever and wherever the occasion arises. If you call yourself a Christian, then you are already appointed to be a witness. Jesus himself decreed it. "...You will receive power when the Holy Spirit comes on you; and you will be my witnesses in Jerusalem, and in all Judea and Samaria, and to the ends of the earth" (Acts 1:8).

Many years ago I was an intern in a large city hospital. I had wrestled for many years with the matter of sharing my faith. I was self-conscious and fearful of offending. Thankfully, so far as my patients were concerned, doctors were not supposed to take advantage of the doctor/patient relationship.

One evening I was struck with the elaborate defenses I had perfected. Without even being aware of what I had been doing, I had developed a clever way of only sharing my convictions when at a psychological advantage. I could sense when "religion" might come up—four conversational steps before it actually did. I would promptly take evasive action by throwing in a "deflector" and turning the conversation in another direction—unless I sensed I could deliver some unanswerable argument.

That evening God showed me both how dishonest and how unloving my behavior had been. I was interested only in looking good, not in being a fellow human being. I determined that from that moment I would try to be simple and honest in my conversations, and forget about looking like a fool. I had to learn to be *real*.

The next morning the first test came as I was conducting the round on the hospital ward. Routinely I asked patients how they were. One patient answered me, "I'm scared, doc. I'm so very scared."

"Is there any way I can help?"

"Do you ever get scared, doc?"

"Sometimes. But I'm not scared at the moment. How can I help?"

"How do I stop being frightened? How could I be like you?"

I could have given any one of a hundred answers. Some would have been platitudes, others standard techniques for dealing with patients facing fear in a strange, hospital setting. But he had implied that I knew something about overcoming fear, and that was true. I forget my exact words. They were something like, "I think I'm not afraid because I have a faith in Jesus."

"Really? You mean—could you tell me about it?"

"Not right now. Let me get back to you this evening." That night changed my patient's life.

What is a witness? Witnesses give truthful evidence of what they know from personal observation. Their function is to answer truthfully to things they know by experience, by having been present. Witnesses are not theorists.

On one occasion Jesus healed a blind man (see the ninth chapter of the Gospel of John). At first, the religious leaders of his day argued that he could not be the same man who had been blind. The man with whom they were presented must look the same, but be a different person. They demanded to see the parents, who agreed that the man was indeed their formerly blind son.

"Then how is it he now sees?" the hostile leaders demanded.

The parents were scared. "He is our son," they replied fearfully, "but we've no idea how he is able to see now. Ask him."

The religious leaders did so. I record the interaction between them and the man who had been blind for two reasons. First, it illustrates the endlessly repeated hostility between firsthand witnesses and those who have a vested interest in not accepting truth. Second, the exchange illustrates what a witness is, even under hostile questioning.

A second time they summoned the man who had been blind. "Give glory to God," they said. "We know this man is a sinner."

He replied, "Whether he is a sinner or not, I don't know. One thing I do know. I was blind but now I see!" Then they asked him, "What did he do to you? How did he open your eyes?"

He answered, "I have told you already and you did not listen. Why do you want to hear it again? Do you want to become his disciples, too?"

Then they hurled insults at him and said, "You are this fellow's disciple! We are disciples of Moses! We know that God spoke to Moses, but as for this fellow, we don't even know where he comes from."

The man answered, "Now that is remarkable! You don't know where he comes from, yet he opened my eyes. We know that God does not listen to sinners. He listens to the godly man who does his will. Nobody has ever heard of opening the eyes of a man born blind. If this man were not from God, he could do nothing."

To this they replied, "You were steeped in sin at birth;

how dare you lecture us!" And they threw him out (Jn 9:24-34).

A witness is like a signpost. Two things are important in a signpost. One is that it point in the right direction; the other, that it be legible. You can have beautiful signposts with ornate lettering. But if they point in the wrong direction, or if the lettering, however beautiful, is illegible—they are useless. The former blind man didn't know much. He had no idea who Jesus was. He was no expert in philosophy or theology, just an illiterate beggar. Yet he knew what had happened to him. And he told the truth.

Truth is not always welcome. Truth in this case would have destroyed the spurious arguments of the religious leaders. They rejected the truth and were enraged with the witness who spoke it. It will always be the same. But there are many who long for the truth that will set them free.

A LIFESTYLE OF CHANGE

You will find it much easier to be a witness if your spiritual renewal is progressing. Once you stop changing, you really stop living. The two aspects of AA's twelfth step are equally important. You will not be an effective carrier of any message unless you are actively carrying out the principles embodied in the message yourself. And if you fail to carry the message to others, you will lose ground in your own process of growth.

We are concerned with ongoing change, the constant change of ongoing personal growth, of developing maturity. Change and repentance are partners, and repentance is a way of life. In the previous chapter I mentioned Charles Colson's view on the matter:

"But the repentance God desires of us is not just contrition over particular sins; it is also a daily attitude, a perspective. Repentance is the process by which we see ourselves, day by day, as we really are: sinful, needy, dependent people. It is the process by which we see God as he is: awesome, majestic and holy.... And [it] so radically alters our perspective that we begin to see the world through God's eyes, not our own. Repentance is the ultimate surrender of the self."[2]

PRESSING THROUGH PAIN

Throughout this book I have made it clear that change and pain are linked. What I must now add is that pain and joy are concommitants of life. The more of life we have, the greater our experience of both joy *and* pain.

When heaven comes, every tear will be wiped away (Rev 7:17). Perhaps then we shall have only the memory of pain. But heaven is not here yet. In the meantime I offer ongoing change, and therefore ongoing repentance and pain.

To choose real change is to choose a greater capacity for life. Repentance is a doorway to life. And life is wrapped in a bundle with pain—something that most of us fear. I am not a masochist, but I have learned to appreciate pain. By this I do not mean that I enjoy pain, but that I understand its role in life.

Let me express it differently. *My capacity for joy corresponds to my capacity for pain.* I cannot have the one without the other. It is a matter of becoming alive. The more alive I am, the more I am exposed to both joy and pain. The more I learn to experience ecstasy, the more deeply I am exposed to life's agonies.

My pains and joys were once entirely egocentric. They were real, but limited. At the time I thought the pains were unbearable, the joys inadequate. All this is changing. In being lifted (at least in some degree) from total self-centeredness, both pains and pleasures are increasing—but then, so is living.

We are offered what people call "a package deal." If I want increased joy, I need more life. If I want more life, I must run the risk of increased pain.

In my progress from non-living to life, I find I must walk through doorways of pain. The initial pain is that of facing reality. As I pass through each successive doorway, I experience an increase in alive-ness, and with it an increased capacity to experience both pleasure and pain. I begin to see the world around me not only in subtler tones, but in starker contrasts. I begin to experience yet more horrendous agonies and yet more exquisite raptures. But having tasted, I want to go ahead, not retreat. Joy pulls me forward.

The choice is between life and death. To choose life is to choose both capacities—for pain and for pleasure, for ecstatic joy and for appalling agony. For myself—with trembling—I opt for life. I want to live, not to remain in death.

Christ offers me life. If life comes wrapped in thorns, then let me seize it! To feel pain is better that to have no feeling at all. And if the thorns are wrapped around "with an inexpressible and glorious joy" (1 Pet 1:8), then, pain or no pain, I must untangle the thorns.

ELEVEN

A New Life for the Old

*...They will soar on wings like eagles; they will run and
not grow weary, they will walk and not be faint.*

Isaiah 40:31

T his book began with the question: Can people change?
First I gave several examples of people who had
done so, who seemed to have changed permanently for the
better. Most of them had changed as a result of some crisis in
their lives. I used as illustrations earthquakes and Japanese
domino exhibitions to show the principles of sudden change.

While it is true that change by earthquake is possible, I
made it clear that gradual change is equally important provided it is permanent, ongoing, and in harmony with reality.
Can people change? The answer is YES. People can change.
They can change for the better. They can change permanently for the better. They can even "grow," mature, and develop emotionally. They can learn a new zest for life.

This is why repentance must be ongoing. Many people
who read this book will have known God for years, but may
not have understood these principles. The spiritual life
within may not have grown and developed as it should
have. Others may have known *about* God—have believed in
his existence, may even have acquired extensive theological
understanding, without having enjoyed a rich spiritual life at

all. Still others may be "beginners," facing these issues seriously for the first time.

Whatever category you may place yourself in, the issue of change-by-repentance is an ongoing issue, offering benefits far greater than any one-time action.

ABOUT LEOPARDS AND THEIR SPOTS

We saw that permanent change has to begin inside a person. The leopard could lose its spots only if its inner nature were to change—a permutation of its genetic code. In the same way, our nature must change from within. Inner change results in outwardly changed behavior. My actions and words will begin to be different because *I* am different. My character and personality will be subtly but clearly altered. I will not be merely acting a part, but will really be a different person.

Can any person change? Let me affirm and reaffirm: yes—and a thousands times over—yes!

Change of this sort comes about by renewed vision—vision imparted to me by God. With fresh eyes I see the truth—the truth about myself, about God, about the universe. It is a new kind of seeing—a seeing with my heart, not just my head. What I see may have a profound effect on me. I may weep, be dismayed, or even be delirious with joy. But if I decide to respond appropriately, that is to say if I repent, I collaborate with God in bringing about change.

The distress of seeing has to do with the discovery that what I thought of as merely a "problem" is in fact an expression of evil. I discover a beast in my own basement. Behavior and attitudes of which I had once been proud—I now face with shame and dismay. Evil stalks ever more arrogantly through the world, and I begin to see that I myself am a part of that evil.

The discovery can be painful—*very* painful. Yet as I act on the vision God imparts to me, my shame and sorrow become a doorway through which I can pass to peace, joy, and new freedom from the enslavement of evil.

Later chapters in the book, particularly chapters eight and nine, dealt with steps a person may take to facilitate that seeing. Inner vision is deeply mysterious. It falls on some people with dramatic, even catastrophic intensity. For others the seeing is a new dawn slowly stealing over the horizon of their night. Meditative self-examination and discussion with friends and helpers all may play a part.

You may have difficulty with the idea of God and the supernatural. In this you are not alone. You will remember that the founders of AA anticipated this resistance with the phrase "God as you understand him." For my part, I suggested an experiment—the examination of the Gospel of John, along with a prayer: "God, if you are there, please reveal yourself to me."

Mine is a taste-and-see approach. But I warned that the approach might not work if you are unwilling to risk the consequences. For the experiment will put you in touch with reality, with the living force and power of the invisible God who created you and who has the right to rule over your life. You may not want that. If you say, "Well, I may have my faults, but at least I should be my own master," then the experiment is ruined from the start.

On the other hand your difficulty may be of a different kind. Sometimes when we say that something is "too good to be true," we say the words cynically, or else with wistful longing. What I have been saying may seem like a beautiful dream. "It would be so lovely *if…*" But on the heels of the "if" comes an unexpressed sigh. If this is so, I can only urge you that when Jesus said, "Come to me, all you who are weary and burdened, and I will give you rest" (Mt 11:28)—he included anyone aware of a problem in their lives for which they crave a solution.

You may feel you are "not important enough" or that

"that sort of thing never happens to me." To the "not important enough," I reply that the God I know weeps over you, longing to gather you into his arms. That is fact, not sentiment. And to the "that sort of thing never happens to me," I respond that this is the time in your life for it to begin to happen.

I travel extensively, even circumnavigating the globe from time to time. I have lost count of the countries I have visited, many of them repeatedly. You must be aware of the sweeping changes, the dissolution of the community experiment, the restlessness and violence that gather momentum even as I write. What rarely gets into the press or television are the religious changes—astonishing revivals of interest in religious matters in almost every country in the world.

It is not just that people everywhere are asking age-old questions about the meaning of human existence, but rediscovering the powers of the world to come right in their midst. I mention it simply because if ever there was a time in human affairs when "this sort of thing" could happen to you, that time is now. We live in the middle of world change and personal change. Primitive people and sophisticated people, famous people and unknown people all over the world are experiencing the changes I have been describing.

Do you feel your case is too hard? Too hard for you, perhaps. Too hard for any human resource. But not too hard for God. I can only say, as a habitual cynic, that I am constantly astonished by the changes God brings about in people.

I think of the once ambitious General Ponce Enrile in the Philippines. This influential general helped to overthrow President Marcos and enable Mrs. Aquino to gain power. Later, frustrated with her administration, he opposed Mrs. Aquino and at one point was arrested and briefly confined to a prison camp.

At some point fairly recently in his tempestuous career, Enrile was challenged by his son to learn what the Bible had to say about the real nature of Christianity. The general began to attend Bible studies in the home of a friend. He experienced repentance. On June 16, 1990, at his first public appearance following this, he made the following statement:

> "It is perhaps correct to say that every true believer in Christianity has an individual encounter with the Lord.... My sins are my own and your sins are your own in a very personal way.... Whether the sins are the same in character or not, they are peculiarly personal to the sinner. And it is the sinner, no one else, who must repent for them. For our Lord Jesus said in Mark 1:15, 'The time has come, the kingdom of God is near. Repent and believe the good news!' ...I found my peace. I have thrown away my worries. I have learned to forgive, even those who persecute me; to be meek, gentle and tolerant to and of others."[1]

Enrile's career had not been noted for forgiveness, meekness, gentleness, or tolerance. But a radical change had taken place in the depths of his psyche. The beast within him sensed the presence of a new master. This is the kind of change God offers—a transformation available to anyone who wants it.

BEGINNING LIFE OVER AGAIN

People often say, "If only I had my life to live over again!" Usually they are thinking, "If I had it to do over again, I would not make the same mistakes." Some people try to start over again by moving to a new area—sometimes abandoning their families and getting a new job.

They may survive desperate loneliness, but their attempts rarely succeed. Why? Because we are the source of most of our problems. Usually the personality and character defects produced in one environment will be reproduced in a new environment. The same problems and mistakes resurface.

Alcoholics refer to this maneuver as the *geographical cure*.

Would things be any different if we could begin life over again from birth? I am neither a fatalist, nor a determinist. However, I recognize that to some extent we are "shaped." We are each more vulnerable to certain sins and follies, more likely to do some things than others. Our upbringing, our culture, our in-born nature all push us in a certain direction. They neither force us nor seal our destinies. We choose, and our choices are real choices. But these realities do make one destiny more probable than another.

Because we can never actually live our lives over again, there is no way of telling what would happen if we could return to the womb and start life all over again. However, beginning with the same genes and the same environment, it is likely that we would turn out much the same way. Experience teaches us lessons we can never apply to the past.

NEW LIFE FOR OLD

God offers us something different, a new life—his own divine life growing and developing inside of us, reproducing God's nature and modifying our own. Such is the possibility to which repentance is a doorway.

But God offers each of us more than new life inside. He gives us a new identity. I remain *me* but a new Me, a me with my own past, but with new personhood and a newly acquired identity to replace my old one. This is the sort of life—a life in two senses—to which repentance can give rise.

This new life and new identity can mean permanent change. How does it work?

We live in a world of science gone mad. Among medical treatments in today's knowledge-glutted world is that of implanting living tissues from unwanted babies in the bodies of sick patients. It is yet one more disturbing development of modern medicine—disturbing not because it fails to work, but because of the moral and ethical dilemmas it raises.

Remains from aborted children abound. Cells from certain parts of the brain of a newly-dead child, for example, can be transferred to the tissues of a patient with, say, Parkinson's disease, to alleviate the humiliating symptoms of shaking and rigidity. Again, cells from the pituitary gland can be used to bring new life where corresponding cells in a sick person's body no longer function.

What we are dealing with is an application of the principle of new life for old, alive life for failing or defective life. Blood transfusions and marrow transplants are further examples of this principle. Doctors use new living material to sustain life—or to replace pathological life.

Primitive people instinctively grasp this as a universal principle, even though their understanding of it may be distorted. For instance, if I were a cannibal belonging to certain tribal groups and I managed to kill a renowned rival, in my joy I might immediately cut out his heart (or his liver) and eat it while it was fresh and warm. I would really be after his spirit, and in this way I would acquire his courage, and his warrior skills. What was once inside him will now dwell inside me.

Thus, whether we are dealing with Western invalids or murderous cannibals, the same principle underlies both therapies—whether either of them really works or not. New life, new health, in some cases even new character are imparted to someone, by a sacrifice, at times in the form of a violent death of a victim.

The principle (if not always its application) is universal. An accident victim's eyes bring sight to a blind man, while her heart alleviates a woman's struggle for breath. The murder of a witch doctor and the drinking of his still-warm blood brings the hope that his magic powers will enter the spirit of the drinker. From the shattered remnants of a developing baby's body comes hope for an aging sufferer. New life for old: the violent death of a victim bringing hope and new strength to the living.

It is an astounding principle, one of incredible power. Some examples represent a noble gift from a dead victim. Others appall us. I can forgive the cannibals—appalling as cannibalism is—more easily than I can forgive my medical colleagues. The cold recycling of waste baby flesh must surely dehumanize the recylers. Nevertheless the principle itself is important. The sacrificial principle of a life given up to give life is as old as humanity itself, whether used cruelly, coldly, or nobly.

God gives new life better than any of us. He neither promotes violent death nor exploits it. He grants us repentance as a gateway to a totally new life. God changes both who we are and what we are. He can change *what* we are by implanting a new nature in us. He wants to change *who* we are by imparting a new identity to us. God is our Father who wishes to adopt us as sons and daughters, with the full privileges of our new position and identity.

True, the deal did involve a violent sacrificial death. There had to be a price tag on so momentous an undertaking, so God chose to suffer the violence and to undergo the death—himself. He achieved our salvation on the basis of a violent death, a human sacrifice *voluntarily suffered*, by Jesus, the God/man.

Let me first comment on the new identity offered to us in Christ. Christianity grew up in the Roman world. The New Testament concept of our adoption by God reflects the Roman law. A wealthy Roman citizen could adopt any man or woman—even a slave—and confer upon that person the full legal rights of his natural children, including Roman citizenship. The adopted son or daughter could actually replace a natural son or daughter, becoming heir to the full inheritance. He would assume a new identity.

The Apostle John, like Paul, comments on the matter;

"How great is the love the Father has lavished on us, that we should be called children of God! And that is what we are!" (1 Jn 3:1).

Let me establish the principle, then, that God offers us a hope beyond our wildest dreams. He not only forgives us, but puts his own life inside our bodies, life that can grow and develop, replacing and expelling the evil tendencies inside of us. Simultaneously we acquire a new identity as children of the Father of all.

This new life and new identity come at the price of a violent death: Christ's own death on a Roman cross two thousand years ago. For the moment, we need not worry about *how* someone's death two thousand years ago can personally affect us after twenty centuries. It is sufficient to grasp that it can. Christ's sacrifice was the price of our pardon and of the new life we may now enjoy.

This new life is the logical consequence of any step of repentance. If you have faith enough to seek the one, you will have faith enough to ask for the other.

BORN INTO A ROYAL HOUSEHOLD

The term "born again" has been cheapened by people who use it glibly, lightly and boastfully claiming kinship with an unearthly family. The new birth of which Jesus spoke was sacred and wonderful. Central to this new life is a relationship with Christ himself. To know Christ is to possess this life. To possess this life is to have personal knowledge of Jesus.

History confronts us with Jesus, the human being no serious historian, *as* a historian, can either ignore or fully understand. The most basic question in life is: do we ignore him, or do we bow to him? Jesus had entered human history by supernatural conception in the body of a peasant girl. He was not merely God inhabiting a convenient body, but had really become a human being.

It is at this point that we react in one of two ways. Either we shake our heads in unbelief, even perhaps in sneering cynicism—or we bow in stunned adoration. We are looking at an event which represents a core Christian belief, along with the crucifixion and the resurrection. It is a core belief not only in the sense that without it there is no Christianity, but also because it tells us what God is like. He was a God who was willing to share our life "from the inside."

Last Christmas we cleared out the fireplace in our living room. First we removed the grate and lined the floor with straw, then carefully arranged figures of shepherds, Joseph, Mary, the infant Jesus, an angel, a cow, and a donkey. The dim illumination of a concealed lamp cast shadows on the soot-blackened walls.

This manger scene formed a fascinating center to the room. I know it probably looked nothing like the actual historic scene, but what held my attention was the wonder of the story it told. For the story was of a God who cares for us, cares so greatly that, "…though he was rich, yet for your sakes he became poor, so that you through his poverty might become rich" (2 Cor 8:9).

If this thought is not ridiculous, then it is absolutely stupendous. We are dealing with a God who cared enough about us to abandon any olympian detachment—cared enough to become a fertilized ovum, to inhabit the same protective warmth of a woman's body, until he became fit enough to emerge and face mortality. And as we stand with the shepherds in a dimly lit stable, amid the dirty straw and the stench of animals and their manure, we should stare at the child.

Thou who wast rich beyond all splendor,
All for love's sake becamest poor;
Thrones for a manger didst surrender,

Sapphire-paved courts for stable floor.
Thou who wast rich beyond all splendor,
All for love's sake becamest poor.

Thou who are God beyond all praising,
All for love's sake becamest Man;
Stooping so low, but sinners raising
Heav'nward by thine eternal plan.
Thou who are God beyond all praising,
All for love's sake becamest Man.[2]

The story is a true story. We are looking at a God who has reduced himself to the helplessness of a newborn baby. The Son of God cannot alleviate his thirst by giving an order, but must nuzzle like any infant, rooting blindly for his mother's breast. Merciful human hands will attend his needs for dryness, cleanness, and comfort. Jesus is reduced to helpless dependency—God, a helpless infant, God incarnate.

But the infant has to grow, and his dawning intelligence will be encompassed by a human brain. He will share our childhood experiences, our struggles with growth, with dawning sexuality, with poverty, with sibling rivalry—with the same equipment we had. He will decide to stand beside sinners in a line of men and women being baptized as penitents, as though he himself were a sinner.

God has subjected himself to self-imposed limitations. He will tolerate no advantage over us other than those that arise from our own sin and stupidity. He is to live his life, he who is still God, through a truly human experience in a real human body. "During the days of Jesus' life on earth, he offered up prayers and petitions with loud cries and tears to the one who could save him from death, and he was heard because of his reverent submission. Although he was a son, he learned obedience from what he suffered and, once made perfect, he became the source of eternal salvation for all who obey him" (Heb 5:7-9).

Jesus learned by experience. He had to be "made perfect" for his life's work. If he was to deliver us from the great curse, he would have to qualify by passing the tests which our forefathers had failed—and in so doing had brought the curse of death upon us.

So, like us, Jesus must find out what it feels like to be tempted. He will therefore face temptation—every kind of temptation a man or a woman can experience. The Son of God never gives way to it. But that only means that he will experience more, not less temptation than we ourselves suffer. After all, we cave in before the pressure is at its height! Jesus will endure temptation to its limit and still not give way—ever.

Thus he will learn obedience through suffering. Thus he will qualify as our champion. "For we do not have a high priest who is unable to sympathize with our weaknesses, but we have one who has been tempted in every way, just as we are—yet was without sin" (Heb 4:15).

RECEIVING THE LIFE AND THE IDENTITY

Just how is this new life imparted to you?

St. John explains more fully; "He was in the world, and though the world was made through him, the world did not recognize him. He came to that which was his own, but his own did not receive him" (Jn 1:10-11).

John was arguing that the man historically known as Jesus was in fact the Creator God. Christ's coming differed from our's in an important way: in being born on earth, Jesus came to territory he already owned. He was the rightful lord of the earth, the lord over everything and everyone in it. Rather than come as a peasant, he could have come as divine judge and destroyed the earth, consumed it.

Instead, Jesus chose to spend nine months in Mary's womb and to experience to the full extent our human condition—all to break the evil curse that lay upon us. As the ultimate man, he bore the full horror of that curse—shattering the power of evil that plagued humanity because of his love for us. In so doing Jesus opened the way to the new life and identity he now offers us.

How do we receive that act of supreme love? How do the new life and identity become our own?

John continues to explain; "He came to that which was his own, but his own did not receive him. Yet to all who received him, to those who believed in his name, he gave the right to become children of God—children born not of natural descent, nor of human decision or a husband's will, but born of God" (Jn 1:11-13).

The new life and new identity hinge on faith. The blessings and benefits of a world to come are for "all who receive" Jesus, "those who believe in his name." To those who receive him and believe on his name he gives "the right to become children of God." They are not merely adopted Roman citizens—but citizens of an age to come, children of the Creator himself. God adopts them, but he does more. In some mysterious manner he sires them. His own life enters into them. They are "born not of natural descent, nor of human decision or a husband's will, but born of God."

The question remains: how does it happen? What does it mean to *receive* Jesus? In what sense is he to be received? And what do the words "believe on his name" mean? We receive Jesus in the same sense that the world rejected him. When he "was in the world," when he "came to that which was his own," Jesus encountered largely a lack of recognition and even outright rejection. Religious leaders viewed him with hostility and murderous hate; the populace offered him fickle admiration; the bewildered civil authorities afforded him no protection, sacrificing him to political expediency. Jesus knew it would happen, predicted the end of his career months before there was any obvious sign of it, and embraced what was to happen for the greater purpose which brought him to live among us.

To receive him we must do the opposite. We are to recognize who and what Jesus truly is—our owner and the lord of our planet. We must bow the knee before him as our rightful lord and master. In this way we reverse what happened historically. If Jesus is who and what he said, we can afford neither indifference nor hostility.

But we need to do more. We "believe in his name." The name Jesus has different spellings according to the human language it is expressed in. In early Hebrew, it was Joshua; in contemporary Hebrew, Yeshua (pronounced Yeh-SHOO-ah); in English, Jesus. The name means rescuer, deliverer, champion, savior.

In dying Jesus championed our cause and paved the way for our salvation. To "believe in his name" is to believe *in what his name means* and to trust him. It is to place our confidence in him and entrust our destiny to him. It is to recognize that Jesus can do for us what his name implies, and to count on him to do so.

Jesus once said, "... whoever comes to me I will never drive away" (Jn 6:37). He wants us to understand that he will always and gladly receive whoever comes to him for help. If this is so, how much greater is the hope of those who come to submit to his authority and count on his power to impart new life.

To be born again is to be "born not of natural descent, nor of human decision or a husband's will, but born of God." This birth is no physiological process, but of a supernatural order—the infusing of supernatural life into our bodies, the life of God himself.

This infusion means that God himself becomes incarnate within us. For what he is offering is more than life, more even than divine life. It is divine life in the form of his very person. God offers us himself—not just a part or a portion of himself, but his whole self. This is a great mystery, I grant you, but one taught by the Bible and the Christian Church down the ages.

RAPE, SEDUCTION, AND WOOING

I must define the relationship carefully. We are called to be in a love relationship that culminates in union. God himself can dwell in us. But he will enter only by our consent. He may urge his suit with passion, but he will not force his will on anyone.

God does not even seduce. He woos. He speaks the truth, reveals the truth, for only by seeing the truth will we be able to make an informed decision.

Our active participation continues in this ongoing relationship for the rest of our lives. Our consent will be required, our trust in him employed in every step along the way. We may—and should—crown him king in our lives. After all, he owns us. But he will never become a tyrant. His rule is gentle, his yoke easy, his burden light.

Nevertheless the difference is profound. For we ourselves will have changed. Once his nature is in us, a new genetic code begins to operate. Our tastes will change. We may still choose evil, and probably will at times. But our hatred of doing so will increase. We will begin to hate things we once loved, discover new beauties in things we once ignored. We will have changed from within. Siding with good will become more natural, more appealing. The pull of evil, though great at times, will progressively diminish over time.

However, it will do so in the degree that we behave in accordance with our true (that is, our *new*) nature. Our true nature is to be a child of the Father. As we relate to him on a daily basis, something within us will develop more and more. We will have become different persons. Formerly turkeys, we will have become eagles. Our wings will grow, our necks shorten, our wattles disappear.

Isaiah told us that placing our hope in God would result in renewed strength. We would run effortlessly, soar on eagle wings.

THE BALL IN YOUR COURT

Give yourself a break. Expand your wings and soar! You can change. Permanently. For the better. From within. You can repent. Or, if you repented long ago, you can move into a life of ongoing repentance. You can learn what real human life is all about.

God himself has paid the price. He will be glad to initiate the process, enter your life, and impart his own nature to you. If he entered long ago, he can now change his relationship with you radically. However incredible the fact may appear, God yearns for intimacy with you. And he wants you to respond.

There is a price, of course. There was for God, and there will be for you. The price is to face the truth—primarily the truth about yourself, your sin, and your helplessness to change matters. It's humiliating, but then, a bit of humility never hurt anybody. In fact it heals. And in any case, who are you or I to keep the Creator of the universe waiting? If anyone has humbled himself it is God—not that pride has ever been a problem with him.

Strange that I should be making a sort of sales pitch, for I have nothing to sell. You've already bought (or borrowed) my book—so I'm out to gain nothing. Paul, the first century missionary, said it long ago when he retold the story of four starving lepers.

The beggars had gone to the camp of an army besieging Jerusalem, since the risk of death by execution seemed preferable to the slow death of starvation. They found the invading army camp empty of soldiers, but full of food and riches. The army had mysteriously fled.

> The men who had leprosy reached the edge of the camp and entered one of the tents. They ate and drank, and carried away silver, gold and clothes, and went off and hid them. They returned and entered another tent and took some things from it and hid them also. Then they said to each other, "We're not doing right. This is a day of good news and we are keeping it to ourselves. If we wait until daylight, punishment will overtake us. Let's go at once and report this to the royal palace" (2 Kgs 7:8-9).

I have good news that I may not, must not keep to myself. My life is still changing. I have found joys that I never thought would be mine, joys that demand expression. I must announce them, spell them out, broadcast them. Paul felt the same way. When he talked about the "gospel," the word for him was synonymous with the expression "good news."

Faced with stoning, imprisonment, dangers and opposition of all kinds, it was a joy-filled sense of obligation to God and his fellow humans that drove Paul to relentlessly announce the good news. "Yet when I preach the gospel, I cannot boast, for I am compelled to preach. Woe to me if I do not preach the gospel!" (1 Cor 9:16).

I feel the same way. This joy-filled sense of obligation is what drives me relentlessly forward. However dark the political and economic skyline, "this is a day of good news." Like the four lepers, I cannot keep silent.

I do not know what you will make of what I have written. I have explained matters (with the help of proficient editors) as well as I can, and you have read what I have written.

Blessings on you! The ball is now in your court.

Notes

ONE

1. John White, *The Golden Cow* (Leicester: InterVarsity Press, 1979), 8-9.
2. I believe that cognitive therapy, a form of treatment employed by psychologists, will produce ongoing effectiveness in the degree that involves far more than cognition. Among other things, it must in some way involve the physiology of emotion and the activity of the right hemisphere of the brain.

TWO

1. Charles W. Colson, *Born Again* (London: Hodder & Stoughton, 1979), 24.

2. Ibid., 23.	7. Ibid., 27.	12. Ibid., 65.
3. Ibid., 24.	8. Ibid., 57.	13. Ibid., 16.
4. Ibid., 22.	9. Ibid., 55.	14. Ibid., 14.
5. Ibid., 22.	10. Ibid., 61.	15. Ibid., 74-75.
6. Ibid., 27.	11. Ibid., 38.	16. Ibid., 89.

17. Depression can arise by different mechanisms and vary widely in severity and form. In Chuck's case it seems to have been a sort of "calm before the storm" repentance. That does not mean, however, that depression is always a sign of the need for repentance!
18. Ibid., 113-114.
19. C.S. Lewis, *Mere Christianity* (London: Fontana, 1954), 59.
20. Colson, *Born Again*, 116-117.

THREE

1. Colson, *Born Again*, 113-114.
2. René Spitz describes his observations in two technical articles in the twenty-five-volume *Psychoanalytic Study of the Child*, ed. Ruth S. Eissler et al. (New York: International Univs. Press, 1945ff), 1:53, 2:213.
3. Harry Harlow, "The Nature of Love," *American Psychologist* 13 (1958), 201-210.
4. See the brief and popular treatment in Earl Wilson, *A Silence to be Broken* (Leicester: InterVarsity Press, 1987).
5. John White, *The Masks of Melancholy* (Leicester: InterVarsity Press, 1982), 111, quoting L. Camille, "Life Events and Depressive Disorders Reviewed," *Archives of Psychiatry*, 37 (1980):529-535 and G.W. Brown, T.R. Harris, and R. Copeland, "Depression and Loss," *British Journal of Psychiatry*, 130 (1977):1-8, and F. Brown, "Depression and Childhood Bereavement," *Journal of Mental Science*, 107 (1969):754-77.
6. For recent developments in the understanding of both male and female homosexuality, see Leanne Payne, *The Broken Image* (Eastbourne, W. Sussex: Kingsway Publications, 1988) and Elizabeth Moberly, *Homosexuality: A New Christian Ethic* (Cambridge, England: James Clarke & Co., 1983).
7. Jim McFadden, "Forgiveness: the Crucial Ingredient," *Pastoral Renewal*, vol. 14, no. 2, 5-6.

8. M. Scott Peck, *The Road Less Traveled* (New York: Simon and Schuster, 1978), 45.

FOUR

1. Jung saw God as a four-in-one being: Father, Son, Spirit, and a fourth member. Sometimes he seemed to view the fourth member as woman, sometimes as evil.
2. Leon Jaworski, *Crossroads* (Elgin, IL: David C. Cook, 1981), 89.
3. Ibid., 100.
4. Malcolm Muggeridge, "The Human Holocaust," in Ronald Reagan, *Abortion and the Conscience of a Nation* (New York: Thomas Nelson, 1984), 87-88.
5. Leo Alexander, "Medical Science under Dictatorship," *New England Journal of Medicine*, 4 July 1949, quoted in Muggeridge, "Human Holocaust," 86.
6. Ritual abuse has to do with the physical and sexual abuse of young children and in some cases the sacrificial murder of young children. Newspaper accounts of the disappearance of young children are nowadays occasionally accompanied by a journalist's speculations about the possibility of ritual sacrifice.
7. Kevin Marron, *Ritual Abuse: Canada's Most Infamous Trial on Child Abuse* (Toronto: McClelland-Bantam, 1988).
8. Robert Louis Stevenson, *The Strange Case of Dr. Jekyll and Mr. Hyde* (London: Collins, Library of Classics), 226-229.
9. Ibid., 79.
10. Ibid., 226-229.
11. C.S. Lewis, *The Lion, the Witch, and the Wardrobe* (London: Collins, 1970), 29.
12. C.S. Lewis, *Mere Christianity* (London: Fontana, 1954), 114.
13. Ibid., 114.
14. Ibid., 108-109.
15. Ibid., 109-110.
16. Victor Hugo, *Les Miserables* tr. Charles E. Wilbour (New York: Simon and Schuster, Pocket Books, 1964), 188.
17. Lewis, *Mere Christianity*, 111.

FIVE

1. C.S. Lewis, *Mere Christianity*, 60.
2. AA and its sister programs focus on two critical factors—honesty with ourselves and others, especially about our utter defeat before something too strong for us, and the need to rely on a power greater than ourselves.
3. Oswald Chambers, *My Utmost for His Highest* (London: Marshall, Morgan & Scott, 1986), December 12.
4. Charles G. Finney, *True and False Repentance* (Grand Rapids, MI: Kregel Publications, 1966), 12.
5. Eugene H. Peterson, "Growth: An Act of the Will?" *Leadership*, vol. 9, no. 4, 34-40.
6. Experts in New Testament Greek tell me that this particular understanding of the middle voice does not hold up well in linguistic study, but that the illustration is certainly theologically sound.
7. William Ernest Henley, "Invictus."
8. Peterson, 40.

9. C.S. Lewis, *Voyage to Venus* (London: Pan Books, 1953), 62.
10. Christians conceive of God as a sort of triple personality—three persons making up one divine being. Clearly there is no equivalent kind of existence that we experience here on planet Earth, so we often have some difficulty grasping the concept. The Holy Spirit is often spoken of as the *third member* of the Trinity, and is the "active" member of the trio, doing the divine work here on the planet. It is important to remember, however, that all three are "members" of the one God.

SIX

1. I am thinking primarily here of *professional* interests. Many, perhaps all, psychoanalysts are exceedingly interested on a *personal* level with issues of morality.
2. Hugo, 75.
3. William Shakespeare, *Richard III*, act 5, scene 3, L. 193. *Complete Works* (London: Collins, 1978), 744.
4. John Bunyan, *The Holy War* (London: The Religious Tract Society, no date), 27-31.
5. The story does not appear in the earliest manuscripts of John's Gospel. Its style reflects the three synoptic Gospels, and it is sometimes attributed to Luke.
6. C.S. Lewis, *The Great Divorce* (London: Collins, 1946), 27-31.
7. John White, *The Race* (Leicester: InterVarsity Press, 1984), 41-43.
8. Bunyan, 114.
9. Bunyan, 115.
10. Hugo, 33-34.

SEVEN

1. *The Confessions of St. Augustine*, tr. Rex Warner (New York: Mentor, New American Library, 1963), 17.
2. *American Journal of Psychiatry*, 143:2, February 1986, 226-229.
3. This account is taken from John White, *The Masks of Melancholy* (Leicester: InterVarsity Press, 1982), 15-17.
4. *The Works of Jonathan Edwards*, vol. 1 (Edinburgh: Banner of Truth Trust, reprinted 1976), 238.
5. Richard Baxter, *The Saints' Everlasting Rest* (Welwyn, Herts: Evangelical Press, 1979), 359.
6. Ibid., 359.
7. Charles G. Finney, *Memoirs of Rev. Charles G. Finney* (New York: A.S. Barnes, 1876), 20.
8. Finney, *True and False Repentance* (Grand Rapids, MI: Kregel Publications), 14-15.
9. Jean LaFrance, *Pray to Your Father in Secret* (Sherbrook, Quebec, Canada: Editions Pauline, 1986), 49.
10. John White and Ken Blue, *Healing the Wounded* (Leicester: InterVarsity, 1985), 143.
11. Francis Thompson, *The Hound of Heaven* (New York: Dodd, Mead and Co., 1962), 60.

EIGHT

1. *Alcoholics Anonymous*, 2nd ed. (New York: Alcoholics Anonymous World Services, Inc., 1955), 59.

2. Source unknown.

3. John White, *The Sword Bearer* (Leicester: InterVarsity Press, 1986).

4. Archaeologists and historians dispute the dates of the invasion. However, there seems to be an increasing tendency to opt for a period in the late Bronze I Age (around 1550-1400 B.C.). See Carl G. Rasmusson, *N.I.V. Atlas of the Bible* (London: Marshall Pickering, 1990), 92-97.

5. See Mrs. Oliphant, *The Makers of Florence* (London: Macmillan and Co., 1897), 274.

NINE

1. Charles Colson, *Against the Night* (London: Publications, 1989), 140.

2. Oswald Chambers, *My Utmost for His Highest* (London: Marshall, Morgan & Scott, 1986), June 14.

3. Frank Laubach, *Practicing His Presence*, Library of Spiritual Classics #1 (Portland, ME: Christian Books, 1981), 6, 7.

4. C.S. Lewis, *Mere Christianity*, 168.

5. Richard Baxter, *The Saints' Everlasting Rest* (Welwyn, Herts: Evangelical Press, 1979), 343.

6. Ibid., 338.

7. Joyce Huggett, *Listening to God* (London: Hodder & Stoughton, 1986).

8. Mark Virkler, *Dialogue With God* (South Plainfield, NJ: Peacemakers Ministries Ltd., 1986), 86.

9. Baxter, 359.

10. Jean LaFrance, 171.

11. Tony Campolo, *The Kingdom of God Is a Party* (Milton Keynes, Beds: Word Publishing, 1990), 5-8.

TEN

1. White, *The Golden Cow*, 8, 9.

2. Charles Colson, *Against the Night* (London: Hodder & Stoughton, 1990), 140.

ELEVEN

1. From a newsletter sent out by Frank and Ginny Doten, missionaries to the Philippines, and friends of the Enriles. The quotations in the letter are from Enrile's first public appearance following his repentance.

2. Bishop Frank Houghton, "Thou Who Wast Rich" from *CAROLS* (Downers Grove, IL: InterVarsity Press), Carol #13.

3. Most biblical scholars seem to agree that Jesus' full knowledge, both of his true identity and of his fatal mission, came to him as he was being baptized by John in the Jordan river (see Mt 3:13-17, Mk 1:12, 13, Lk 4:1-13). The voice from heaven echoes two Bible passages, Psalm 2:7 and Isaiah 42:1, speaking of his sonship and of his identity with the suffering servant who would die for the sins of the people. See James Denney's helpful treatment of the subject in the first chapter of *The Death of Christ* (New Canaan, CT: Keats Publishing, Inc.), 13-16.

4. Jesus is speaking: "No one knows about that day or hour, not even the angels in heaven, nor the Son, but only the Father" (Mt 24:36). See also Mk 13:32.